Peter Gwinn

with additional material by
Charna Halpern

Group
Improvisation

The manual of ensemble improv games

mp

MERIWETHER PUBLISHING LTD.
Colorado Springs, Colorado

Meriwether Publishing Ltd., Publisher
PO Box 7710
Colorado Springs, CO 80933-7710

Executive editor: Theodore O. Zapel
Assistant editor: Renée Congdon
Cover design: Jan Melvin

© Copyright MMIII Meriwether Publishing Ltd.
Printed in the United States of America
First Edition

Library of Congress Cataloging-in-Publication Data

Gwinn, Peter Campbell, 1971-
  Group improvisation : the manual of ensemble improv games / by Peter Campbell Gwinn ; with additional material by Charna Halpern.
    p. cm.
  ISBN 1-56608-086-X
1. Improvisation (Acting) I. Halpern, Charna, 1952- II. Title.
  PN2071.I5G9 2003
  792'.028--dc21

                            2003004865

        1 2 3   03   04   05

Dedication

This book is dedicated to the late Del Close, who taught me what group work is all about; to the improv teams Faulty Wiring, Baby Wants Candy, and The Chicago 8, three groups that gave me the joy of being part of a true ensemble; and to my wife Emily. Our team is pretty fun to be on, too.

Contents

Foreword

I was hired a number of years ago to lead an ice-breaking seminar for two companies that had just been involved in a merger. These people would be meeting for the first time and the CEO had the idea that a workshop in improvisation would be an effective way to begin things.

When I arrived with my team of facilitators from ImprovOlympic, we were told that our clients were having some arguments in a meeting and that they would get to us soon. Half an hour passed, and we were told that there were still heavy arguments going on — hopefully they would be ready for us in a little while. Another half-hour passed with no resolution to the arguments. Finally, we got someone to interrupt and ask the CEO to let us step in and see if we could alleviate the tension. To his credit, he let us.

We walked into a hostile environment. After a brief speech to lighten the mood a bit, we got the businessmen to agree to try some exercises and go back to their discussion group later. Already I knew that this workshop would be a huge success. And I was right! By getting them to agree on something — anything — we opened the lines of communication among them. They started working and playing together instead of arguing. While there were still moments of hostility, they were tempered by humor and were easier to accept. By the end of the workshop, even this group, our toughest audience, was able to learn successful team-building, the art of listening, and negotiating so that everyone wins.

Seriously, that CEO was right to call on us. The ImprovOlympic theater is world famous for its mastery of strong teamwork and for creating an environment that is rooted in trust, support, and agreement. It is this environment that creates great improvisational ensembles. A group of performers who trust that they will support one another can take great risks together to achieve great art. The skills of improvisation that make successful ensembles can also help any group work better together. The wise CEO that I mentioned before knew this, which is why he hired I.O. to do the seminar for them. Even an angry boardroom can become a healthy work environment. These skills enable our corporate clients to strengthen their team-building, communicate effectively, and gain a distinct edge in the corporate arena.

Of course, any group can benefit from increased communication, not just improv teams and corporations, which is the reason Peter Gwinn has written this book. Peter is one of ImprovOlympic's top directors and performers. He has taught classes and led workshops for I.O. for years, and is the perfect person to reveal some of our secrets.

When warming up a team before a show or helping a class full of strangers get comfortable with each other, our teachers and coaches have a number of exercises and games that heighten awareness, break the ice, increase concentration, and wire the brains together. Peter has pulled these resources together in this book in a way that will be effective for theater groups, corporations, classrooms, and marriages.

Improvisation is an invaluable tool that has immediate results and lasting effects, no matter what the environment. Hopefully, this book will entice you to learn more.

— Charna Halpern
April 2002

Preface

Some of these games were invented by me. But a lot of them weren't. Even the ones I think I made up were probably also made up by somebody else in some other group. In the improvisational world, games and exercises are like folktales, passed down from generation to generation as oral history. I have collected as many of these as possible in this book to give them permanence and to help them spread beyond the people who take a class or workshop from me or from whoever taught them to me, so that as many people as possible can benefit from them.

I would like to thank all of the improv teachers of the world, everyone whoever passed on, made up, or modified an improv game. I thank you for your contributions, and I offer you my own. Let's continue to spread the philosophy of "Yes And" until we one day take over the world.

Either that or I'll use my weather-controlling ray.

Chapter 1
An Introduction to Mind Reading

Baby Wants Candy, the resident company of ImprovOlympic in Chicago (and the team with which I perform), recently improvised a musical called "The Hands of Time Are Choking Me." The title was suggested by the audience. For an opening number, all of the members of the group went out on-stage as clocks. The clocks sung the opening number, of which the chorus was "Repetition, doing the same thing over and over." The first scene featured me, as an old clockmaker, Ali, as my daughter, and Stuart, as a handsome young customer. When Ali first saw Stuart and acted like she had fallen in love, I decided, for no particular reason, that my daughter fell in love with all the handsome male customers. So my first line of the scene was "Here we go again."

The musical continued; it was forty-five minutes long. The plot included a dying father trying to capture a tiger for his children, two wooden figures from a cuckoo clock trying to escape, and a clock that could make time go in reverse. At the end of the piece, when the tiger killed one of the dying father's children, Ali activated the clock that could reverse time. We did the whole show backwards, like rewinding a video. We went back in time to before the first scene of the show and prevented the father from contracting his fatal disease. Having solved the biggest problems, time went forward again. Replaying the first scene of the show, I said my first line, "Here we go again," and it had an entirely different meaning. The wooden figurine realized it was still stuck in the clock and had to escape all over again, and the cast reprised the opening number: "Repetition, doing the same thing over and over."

How could we have known at the beginning of an improvised show that we would be repeating entire scenes? What made me say "Here we go again" instead of "Oh, no. My daughter always falls in love with the customers?" We couldn't have known ahead of time what we were going to do. But we could realize what possibilities were created by what we had done. Two things happened in that show: We perfectly set up a time loop without knowing that a time loop was going to happen, and once we made a time loop happen, we used the stuff we had set ourselves up with. One of us alone could not have pulled this off. Each one of us going off separately and bringing our ideas together couldn't have pulled it off. The only way this show was able to happen was by all of us working together as a group, never trying to pull the group in a specific direction, but following and building on what the group had already done. By following and supporting whatever came out, we were able to build a whole far greater than the sum of its parts. This phenomenon is an example of the Group Mind.

The Group Mind is the Holy Grail of improvisation. It is the magic part of improvisation. It is the moment on-stage when the improvisers suddenly know what each other will do before they do it. It's like ESP. I can then set you up for a joke with full confidence that you will provide the punch line. Likewise, you have the punch line at the ready, because before I've said it, you know that the setup is coming. Experiencing the Group Mind once will keep improvisers coming back for years.

Improvisers are not the only ones who experience the Group Mind. You can see it on a football field, where the quarterback knows which way the wide receiver is going to turn. You can find it on fire brigades, where firefighters know where each one of them should go, without having to say it. You can even find it in a couple who see something on the street and both think of the same memory at the same time, looking at each other and laughing when they realize they don't have to actually speak.

An established Group Mind is like an out-of-body experience. Suddenly, you can see that you are not just you, but are a part of a greater entity. You feel a sense of excitement, a sense of belonging, and a sense of importance. A team that can achieve the Group Mind will do great group work.

This book exists to help your group achieve the Group Mind. Of course, the best way to achieve the Group Mind is to work together closely for five years. Then, you'll be reading each other's minds like an old married couple. However, I realize that a tragically small number of plays have a five-year rehearsal period. And your boss rarely comes into a meeting to announce "You four are teamed up on this project. I'll need to see your report in five years." So, the exercises in this book are designed to help your group along to the Group Mind. They will speed along your progress toward the Group Mind, or, in the language of normal people, they will assist with group bonding.

"Group bonding" is synonymous with "morale-building." And group bonding is necessary for you to get the best production out of your group. I've been a member of many different kinds of groups: improv teams, sports teams, the cast of a play, a family, a bunch of co-workers in an office. Without fail, the groups that work the best together are groups in which each member feels excited to be a part of the team, feels like they belong on the team, and feels like an important part of the team. Those three characteristics add up to "morale."

Chapter 2

Building Team Spirit
(or Showdown at the OK Morale)

"Morale" is a buzzword — it's tossed around a lot, and has lost its meaning. So I'm giving it its meaning back. Once again, morale is defined as:

1) Each group member feels excited to be a part of the team,
2) Each member feels like they belong on the team, and
3) Each member feels like an important part of the team.

To accomplish 1), you need to create the sense that the team's process is fun, their goals are important, or both. To accomplish 2), you need to ensure that each member has the respect of the other members. Everyone in the group has equal standing. To accomplish 3), you must make sure that each team member makes contributions to whatever it is you're working on.

No matter what the project, a group with high morale is going to enjoy doing the task. Sometimes they'll have fun; sometimes they won't have fun, but they will have the sense of accomplishment that comes from conquering an unpleasant task together. A bonded group enjoys working together, regardless of what it is they're working on.

High morale is the goal of every organization. When people enjoy working together, the results of the work they do are always better. That statement is general — the "work" is "better" — because it applies to so many specific situations. Workers in an insurance office with high morale will pore through mountains of statistics to generate a report without grumbling about the drudgery of the task. The cast of a play will give just a little more during rehearsal. That consultant will stay until seven to finish a project because she wants to, not because she has to. Workers with high morale go that extra step. Their work is more efficient and more inspired. They give more of themselves to their tasks just because they like doing it.

Conversely, workers with low morale don't get much done at all. They spend more time complaining about the work they have to do than they spend actually doing the work. Every new request of them is met with a reason why they can't do it. These are the workers that show up late, that add ten minutes to their lunch, and who start cleaning their desks off at four forty-five to make sure they don't have to stay one second past five o'clock.

So, you want your group to have high morale. The stuff in this book will help. It will also help to know why this book will help. So here is some theory behind morale.

The enemy of high morale is cynicism.

That's "cynicism," not "criticism." Some criticism can be constructive, if it comes from the standpoint of a person who really wants your project to be as good as it can be. Other criticism is destructive; that criticism is fueled by cynicism.

Workers become cynical when their leaders fail to meet their expectations. A failed expectation could be anything from "The boss said he'd give us our assignments three weeks before the deadline, not two," to "The director said we'd never have to stay past ten o'clock" to "Company picnic canceled." Eventually, a group will lose faith in their leadership. When that happens, look out. You are about to face the weapon of the cynic: Judgment.

Judgment comes from a worker who no longer trusts that the actions of his leaders are beneficial to the company or group. The worker, in effect, decides that he knows more about what should be done in the situation than the leader does. So when a directive comes down, the worker will decide if it's what he would do in the situation; if it's not, then chances are he won't do it. And in my experience, there is no greater look of judgment than the one you get when you tell a cynical employee that they're going to spend the afternoon playing improv games. This leads us to lesson two:

Morale is much easier to build than to rebuild.

If at all possible, make the first order of business with your new group be to bond them together. If there is loyalty to a group, then future problems will be met and solved as a group, with each member doing what is needed to solve the problem. If there is no loyalty to the group, then problems result in defensiveness and finger pointing, accompanied by a loss of faith in leadership. When a group first gets together, there is natural excitement and enthusiasm. So the timing is perfect to jump in with some bonding exercises.

If you are trying to rebuild morale using these exercises, I suggest trying to trick them. Tell them that you're just doing this for fun. Tell them they can all be Wayne Brady for a day. Wait until they are having fun, and then tell them that this stuff actually applies to their work.

Much of the descriptions of "groups" up until now have been very general. The reason for the general descriptions is that any group can benefit from these exercises, whether you work for a theater company or a consulting firm. From here on out, the explanations are going to focus a little bit on theatrical groups. Those of you who are more corporate, please translate this into your own vernacular. The reason I have to focus on theater-types is lesson three:

Theater people are the most judgmental people in the universe.

I'm just kidding, of course. No I'm not. The theatrical world is a highly competitive one, and as such, it is only natural that people look for reasons why they are better than others. The extreme end of the spectrum is the breed of theater-type that longs for nothing less than their own separate dressing room with a star on the door and a plate of Oreos pre-twisted apart, the ability to get seated immediately at fancy restaurants, and a personal assistant to abuse. But this also applies to any person who will compliment you to your face and bad-mouth you behind your back.

Even in the theater, the best groups are the ones in which everyone is treated equally. Even though the star may have more lines, you want the person with the smallest supporting role to feel as if they are vital to the show's success. You also want the star to feel that the person with the smallest supporting role is vital to the show's success. A couple show-biz anecdotes to illustrate my point:

A friend of a friend of a friend (let's face it, this story might just be an urban legend) named Judy had a small role in *Hello, Dolly* with Carol Channing on Broadway. One night, during one of Carol's scenes, Judy added a little bit off to the side of the stage that got a laugh. After the show, as legend has it, Carol called Judy into her dressing room and asked her what the name of the show on the marquee was.

"*Hello, Dolly.*" Judy said,

"That's right," replied Carol, "it's not *Hello, Judy*; it's *Hello, Dolly*. Pull that again and you're fired."

Judy was understandably a little miffed by this treatment. After all, isn't it good when people laugh at a comedy? Does it really matter who is getting the laughs? After this incident, Judy went back out and did her bit again, just out of spite. Judy's behavior was a reaction to an unsupportive atmosphere.

An *actual* friend of mine was an extra on an episode of *Star Trek: Voyager* in which she had to stand near a dry ice smoke machine for long periods of time. The guest star of this episode was Sharon Lawrence, fresh off of *NYPD Blue*, so she was a fairly big name. Sharon noticed that my friend's foot was turning blue from being so close to the fog machine. My friend, only being an extra, didn't feel like she could really say anything. But Sharon demanded that they stop shooting and attend to my friend's foot. She behaved as though every last person on set was as important as she was. The result of this was that my friend was very happy to go back to work and also speaks very highly of Sharon Lawrence.

These examples show how morale can be built and maintained by behaving as though everyone is important. A focus of every one of these exercises is that they all must be completed as a group. No one person can take the lead or become more important. So, after working your group through these exercises in which:

Everyone is equal;
Everyone has to contribute; and
Everyone (hopefully) has fun,

You should be well on your way to having a group that loves to work together!

Chapter 3
The Games and Their Explanations

These games and exercises will help your group develop good chemistry. Group Chemistry has many different components. I've come up with a few big ones, which are also the section headings:

Awareness

Good group work builds ideas on top of other ideas. Anything that any member of the group brings to the table can be brilliant. Awareness exercises help a group not only build on the ideas that people offer up, but also to catch the ideas that people bring without knowing it. Awareness can save the planet, according to this exchange from the movie *Independence Day*:

> JUDD HIRSCH AS JEWISH GRANDPA: "Just be careful and don't catch cold."
> JEFF GOLDBLUM AS JEFF GOLDBLUM: "What did you just say?"
> HIRSCH: "Be careful."
> GOLDBLUM: "No, after that."
> HIRSCH: "Don't catch cold."
> GOLDBLUM: "Don't catch cold ... that's it!"

These exercises also allow each member of the group to know what each of the other members are doing at any given time, which is a very practical skill to have. This skill could manifest itself as anything from "Everyone is working on something else, and no one has made these copies yet, so I'll make the copies" to "Joe has something to say, so I won't start talking."

Awareness exercises put the group in tune with each other.

Bonding

These games help a group first get to know each other and then get to trust each other. It's impossible to have a productive group without trust. Alison may have the greatest idea in the world to solve the group's problem, but she won't voice her idea if she's afraid that Neil is going to make fun of it. A large part of Bonding exercises involves putting everyone on equal footing, so that no one stands in judgment of anyone else. The other main part of Bonding exercises is getting the group to complete difficult tasks together. Showing a group that they work well together is ten times as effective as telling them.

Creation

This is largely an area of confidence-building. In a Creation exercise a group will, well, create something together. Usually, it's something simple like a poem or a short story. The result is a product that could not have been made by one person alone. If a group can successfully create some little things together, they'll feel stronger when asked to build something large.

Dynamics

Although in a perfect group, everyone is equal, it doesn't mean that no one ever leads. Rather, everyone in the group needs to take turns being a leader and being a follower. Dynamics exercises help people learn when they need to take the lead and when they need to support the lead of someone else.

Energy

AKA the First Meeting after Lunch exercises. A tired group is a black hole of productivity. Even one really tired guy can drag the energy level of the rest of the group down. Tired people aren't generally excited to do more work. So these exercises are designed to get the blood flowing, get the energy pumped up, and to get a group having fun together, so they become excited to work together.

Focus

There are plenty of distractions in the world. For example, I started to write this book in 1987. I'm just now getting around to finishing it. A group works best when all of its members are giving their full attention to the issue at hand and not the next issue or the last issue or what's for dinner tonight or where their car keys are or the hot/creepy guy/girl from the elevator. These exercises bring the group's mental energy together to a single point of focus. Most of the Focus exercises are concentration games. Some others add the element of layered thinking. When people have to address someone by a different name than normal, or do the opposite of what they're being instructed, it forces them out of their comfort zone of thought. ("Comfort zone of thought," though not particularly catchy, is the best alternative I could come up with to "thinking outside the box." I detest this expression, for I do not believe that I am in a box.) This can free one's mind, so to speak, opening up new approaches to problems.

Most of these games and exercises actually focus on more than one of these categories. They are grouped according to what I feel is the primary focus of the games. I have indicated when there is some overlap.

Although the initials of the categories are ABCDEF, they are presented in the best order for a group that has just come together — BFACED, as in, "These are the challenges your group will 'B FACED' with."

You should also now have the power that comes from knowing that no joke you make doing these exercises can possibly be worse than that "B FACED" pun.

There is also a seventh set of games that all involve overlap:

Party Games

These games incorporate several of the above categories. While they build many aspects of group chemistry at the same time, their primary goal is to be fun. Most of these games I played in some church youth group or something. I use these games in class basically as rewards.

There are some other aspects of group work that these games address. They are:

Breaking the Ice

The group gets comfortable with each other. Members of the group get to know a little more about each other, so they have a little more ground on which to relate. Especially good for new groups, but any group can benefit.

Agreement

The group says "Yes, and" instead of "No, but." The key tenet of improvisation, these exercises teach that it is more productive to agree with an idea and build upon it than to deny an idea and push forth one of your own instead.

Listening and Support

A group absorbs each suggestion and builds upon it, so that every suggestion, even if not a part of the finished product, is at least evaluated. There are two results of Listening and Support: first, everyone feels as though their ideas are important; second, building on each other puts multiple brains to work on the same idea. Six brains working on one solution will develop a better result than six brains working on six solutions.

Teamwork
Every member of the group has to work together to achieve the goal. Disagreeing or promoting your own idea instead of following the group will cause these exercises to fail. Everyone is equally important.

Quick Thinking
Group members: 1) learn to respond quickly, and more importantly, 2) learn to respond decisively, putting their idea out on the table to be worked with, instead of over-thinking and self-censoring until their idea becomes worthless.

Having Fun
Do not underestimate the beneficial impact of doing things just for fun. It creates the equation work=fun in your team's head, which makes them keep coming back.

Now that you know what we're doing, let's just agree how we're going to do it.

Chapter 4

The Secret Code Club for Cool Kids
(Do not skip this chapter)

When I demonstrate these games in classes and workshops, it's much easier, because the people to whom I'm explaining the game can see me. I am thus able to use a series of gestures and indications to clarify my words. In this book, I don't have that luxury. So instead, we're going to develop our own special language, a "secret code," if you will, that will be known only to those who buy this book and read this chapter. Our special secret code will make it easier for me to describe and for you to understand how these games work. Do not reveal the special top-secret code words to anyone, especially people who skip over this chapter. Those people, who are in such a hurry or consider themselves "above" reading chapters labeled "Do not skip this chapter," are people we don't want in our secret code club.

Here are some terms and how we will use them.

It's hard to keep people straight in some of the games that involve large groups. Having a bunch of player ones and twos and first players and other players can get a bit rough. Here is how we will simplify these descriptions. In almost all of these games, a single player starts things off. In all of these game descriptions, that player will be named Doug. So when you see the name Doug, you know that he represents the first player. In your actual group, it's OK if you don't have anyone named Doug. Or if you do have a Doug, he doesn't have to start every game. In fact, I recommend that every time you use a game, you have a different first player. So Doug, you're off the hook.

Frequently in these games, Doug will pass the focus to another individual. In these descriptions, that person will be named Karen. Again, this doesn't mean that Doug always has to go to the same person. Doug and Karen are metaphorical people, representing the first and second people to be involved in your game.

Any other names I use are names of people I know, who are used so their names can be in a book. If you know me and you are wondering, for instance, if you are the Don I had in mind when I named a character Don, the answer is yes.

Most of these games start with the players standing in a circle. Some of the games start with all of the players in a circle except one, who is in the center of the circle. This can get a little confusing, what with people in a circle and also within the circle. So, we will use different terms for the two different situations:

Fig. 1

When the players are in a circle and there is no one in the middle, we will simply say that each of these players is "in the circle."

Fig. 2

When the players are in a circle and there is someone in the center, we will say that the person in the middle is "in the middle of the circle," or simply "in the middle." To avoid using the word "in" anymore, we will say that the other players are "on the outside of the circle."

We will also use "steppers" as a code word for "shoes." This code word has no application to the exercises in this book, and that makes it twice as cool.

Now that we're clear on how to describe these games, let's get to the good stuff.

Games

Bonding

These games are great for a group working together for the first time. They accomplish all of the basic things you need to accomplish to get a group comfortable with each other and working productively.

The most basic game in this chapter is The Name Game, which is a way to learn everybody else's name disguised as a mental exercise. After that, there are two species of games in this chapter: games that have the group achieve a daunting task together, which teaches them how to work as a group, and games that force group members to open up to each other by revealing information about themselves or by showing a willingness to look silly in front of the group, which builds trust in a group.

Both of these types of games are valuable. During a problem-solving exercise, group members are not only completing the assigned task, but are also observing how each other thinks and works: who takes a leadership position, who can see the big picture, who can dispel tension with a joke. By learning how each other works, the group will learn how to work well together.

Trust-building exercises build the group's confidence in itself. The group learns that they can open up to each other without getting made fun of. Once that lesson is learned, the group members will be willing to take risks, to try things that they otherwise might not, secure in the knowledge that the rest of the group will support them if the risk fails.

By the end of these exercises, a group should have the swagger that accompanies the knowledge that they can do whatever they want to and have fun doing it together.

1. The Name Game

Players Needed: 6 or more
Points of Concentration: Breaking the ice, focus and concentration

This is a good game for, obviously, learning each others' names. For that reason, this is usually one of the first exercises I do with a new group. Levels 1 and 2 of this game go together; then you can add 3A or 3B if you want to.

LEVEL 1

Everyone stands in a circle. Doug starts by saying **his own name** and pointing at someone else in the circle. The person pointed to then points at someone else, again saying their own name. Repeat this pattern until everyone has had a chance to hear everyone else's name several times. Then go on to Level 2.

LEVEL 2

Now comes the tricky part. Keep the dynamic of passing the focus around the circle by pointing, but this time when people point, they are going to say the name of the person **at which they are pointing**. Names may still be a little shaky at this point, so I usually add a rule that if someone points at you and says a name that's not yours, just politely tell the person who pointed at you your correct name, take the focus and continue by pointing at someone else.

Choose 3A or 3B for your group.

LEVEL 3A

This level is almost the same as The Yes Game (page 21). The play is similar to Level 2, but instead of pointing to someone when you say their name, you will go take their place in the circle. They will have to say someone else's name so they can vacate their spot to make room for you. There's a little more pressure involved when someone's coming at you than when they're just pointing.

LEVEL 3B

This option stresses learning names less and concentration more. First, the circle sets a rhythm (or "beat") for themselves by snapping. One player starts by saying his name on one snap and someone else's name on the next snap. The person named on the second snap must then do the same thing, starting on the very next snap: their name, then someone else's.

Example:

DOUG: Doug, Nick
group: (snap) (snap)

NICK: Nick, Mary
group: (snap) (snap)

MARY: Mary, Al
group: (snap) (snap)

And so on. If someone misses the beat, says the name of someone who's not there, says the wrong name first, etc., you can just start over or come up with a suitable punishment. For examples of punishments, see the similar game George (page 82).

2. The Yes Game

Players Needed: 6 or more
Points of Concentration: Breaking the ice, agreement

All of the players stand in a circle. Before you start, go around the circle and have everyone say their name. The point of the game is to always have a person moving to take someone else's spot in the circle. Before someone can leave their own spot, they must receive permission from another player to take their spot. Players ask permission to take someone's spot by saying that person's name.

Example:

Doug wants to take Karen's spot in the circle. So Doug says, "Karen?" Karen replies,"Yes." Because this is The Yes Game, she has to say yes. Doug now leaves his spot and heads toward Karen's spot.

Now Karen needs to get out of her spot. She can't leave until someone says "yes" to her, so she asks Ali by saying, "Ali?"

Ali says "yes" to Karen, then "Stuart?" to Stuart. When Stuart says "yes" to her, Ali heads for Stuart's spot. And so on.

The most common mistake people make in this game is to leave their spot in the circle before receiving a "yes," which leaves them stranded in the middle of the circle with nowhere to go. Players who do this are to be laughed at.

If a player looks at someone and addresses them by the wrong name, that person should simply correct the player, and then immediately say "yes."

This is a great game to help a group (or a group leader) learn everyone's names. It also, more importantly, exercises a muscle of agreement in your brain. Having a circle of people all saying "yes" to each other creates a basis of support and trust that can get any group activity off to a good start.

3. Blind Lift

Players Needed: 5 or 6 if a couple are pretty strong and/or
   no one is really big; 7 or more otherwise
Other Needs: Space outside or a room with a high ceiling,
   preferably without a ceiling fan or chandelier
Points of Concentration: Group bonding, working together

The group forms a circle with one lucky volunteer in the middle. The person in the middle must close their eyes and cover up whatever they don't want touched. Once their eyes are closed, the group silently picks a number. The group then starts to count, out loud, up to the secret number. When they reach the secret number, the group will, all together, lift the center person straight up in the air as they say the number.

When I say, "all together," that means that every single person in the circle should be supporting some of the weight of the person being lifted. If everyone has a hand on the person, a group can lift ant-like amounts of weight. By that I mean the proportional amount of weight an ant can lift, not the weight of an ant. I have seen some mighty heavy people be shot right up there by a group of six or seven people working together.

Once you have lifted the person (they should remain vertical the whole time they're in the air), hold them up there for a couple seconds so they can open their eyes and appreciate the view, then set them back down on their feet. Then, they rejoin the circle and someone else goes in the middle. The group decides a different secret count for this person and starts the count. Keep going until everyone's had a turn in the middle.

Faking out the person in the middle is encouraged; something like this usually works: "one, two, three, FOUR, five, SIX, seven, eight ... (lift) NINE!" And on four and six someone would grab an arm or something. I myself have been made to suffer a thirty-count. And a zero-count, for that matter.

This game is one of my favorites, because it amazes a group to see how easily they can lift, like, a two hundred pound guy when they all work together. Also, the group can have a lot of fun together playing with each other's minds.

4. The Knot

Players Needed: 6 or more
Points of Concentration: Group bonding, working together

Everyone stands in a circle, reaches one arm into the center of the circle (it doesn't matter which arm), and takes someone else's hand. Then, everyone reaches their other arm in and takes someone else's hand. No one should hold both hands of the same person. The group will now be in a big knot. The goal of the game is to unravel the knot without letting go of each others' hands. This task requires a lot of teamwork, as people will have to step over or under each others' arms and move around so that others can get over or under their own arms.

Almost every possible knot can be unraveled. Usually, when the knots are undone, the group will be in a big circle. People may be facing in or out of the circle. Sometimes, the group will form two circles, either linked or separate. Part of the fun of the game is finding out what the unraveled shape looks like!

Some of these knots have taken half an hour to undo, but again, they can usually be unraveled. Sometimes, they can't. If that happens, just let people let go and start over. I've never seen two impossible knots in a row.

5. Chain Transformation

Players Needed: 4 or more
Points of Concentration: Group bonding, support

The group stands in a circle, except for one person (Doug) who is in the middle of the circle. Doug starts a repetitive motion and sound. The sound and motion can be something specific (like hammering a nail saying "Bang! Bang! Bang!") or not (hopping from foot to foot, waving your hands over your head and shouting "Widdle woop woop! Widdle woop woop!"). All that is important is that the sound and motion be repetitive so that they can be easily copied.

Once Doug has settled on a sound and motion, he will go up to someone on the outside of the circle and face her, still repeating his sound and motion. The person on the outside of the circle must then mirror Doug, copying the sound and motion exactly. Once Doug is satisfied that the person on the outside is matching his sound and motion, the two of them trade places.

There is now a different person in the middle of the circle doing the first person's sound and motion. So this new person needs to transform the sound and motion into their own sound and motion. By "transform" the sound and motion, I mean that the shift from one to the other should be gradual. A player shouldn't just drop one motion and start another

23

that they had in their head; they should start with the one they are given and change it slowly, seeing where it will lead. Once the second person has established a new sound and motion, they will pass to a third person, who will mirror, trade places, and transform again.

Part of the point of this exercise is that the person in the middle of the circle should look a little stupid. And, perhaps, feel a little stupid. This is intentional. The point is that everyone on the outside of the circle is there for the person in the middle, ready to back them up by looking just as dumb. In fact, when the last person is in the middle of the circle, I like to have the entire circle pick up the sound and motion in a true display of support. The group should learn from this to not be afraid to contribute, because even an idea that makes you look silly will be supported.

Of all of the games in this book, this is the one that is most likely to be played half-heartedly. It's obvious why; you're asking a group of relative strangers to hop around in front of each other shouting "woop woop." Incidentally, the more familiar your group is with each other, the more they will commit to this game. When I do a workshop for a group I haven't worked with before, I will usually make them do this game. I learn all I need to know about how comfortable the group is with each other by whether the group members will play the game in order to not look stupid or whether they play the game to try to make each other laugh. If they're trying to make each other laugh, it means that they trust each other enough that they're not worried about being laughed *at*. Then I know I can do some more advanced stuff.

Your group is playing timidly if the players are entering the circle, transforming the action, and passing it again in fifteen seconds. And they usually have a look on their faces like "Get me out of here!" If this is happening with your group, try this variation on Chain Transformation.

DOUBLE CHAIN TRANSFORMATION

The basic structure is the same until a player gets into the center of the circle. Then, so to speak, we are going to put a landing in the middle of the staircase.

Karen has mirrored Doug and is now in the middle of the circle doing Doug's sound and motion. She must now transform Doug's sound and motion to a new sound and motion. At this point, however, instead of passing to the circle, she must transform her own new sound and motion, in a different way than she did before.

Volume, speed, size, intensity, familiarity, which parts of the body you're using, etc., all describe some different aspects of a sound and motion that can be changed.

Example:
Karen starts off with Doug's motion, which is clapping her hands over her head, saying "Oh yeah! Oh yeah!" She starts to transform, lowering her hands to in front of her face, slowly switching from clapping to a swimming motion. As she does this, the "Oh yeah"s become "Oo-hoo!"s. She holds this new sound and action for a couple seconds.

Now she "takes a right turn." Karen thinks, her first transformation changed the appearance and height of the sound and action, but not the rhythm or volume. So she now transforms a second time, by slowing down her actions and getting quieter. The new speed and sound leads her to put her hand on her hips, stepping from left foot to right foot, whispering, "Hoo. HAH! Hoo. HAH!" She now passes this sound and action to someone on the outside of the circle.

This variation has gotten great results for me. The second transformation forces them to stay out there longer, so they spend more time at-risk. Also, by adding the instruction that the second transformation has to be different than the first, you make players focus a little more on what they're doing and less on how silly they look.

6. Neighbors
Players Needed: 6 or more
Points of Concentration: Group bonding, breaking the ice, energy

The group stands in a circle with one person (Doug) in the middle. Doug, from the middle of the circle, chooses a person on the outside of the circle and asks them, "Do you like your neighbors?" The options for the response to the question are "No" or a "Yes, but" statement.

If the person on the outside says "No," that person's neighbors — who are the people to either side of him in the circle — must change places. When they do, the person in the middle of the circle must try to take one of their places. Like musical chairs, the one who winds up without a place in the circle must now be in the middle of the circle to ask someone else, "Do you like your neighbors?"

If the person on the outside decides he does like his neighbors, he must decide what kind of people he doesn't like. If he decides he doesn't like people with glasses, he will respond to the person in the middle, "Yes, I like my neighbors, but I don't like people wearing glasses." At this point, everyone in the circle who *is* wearing glasses must switch places with each other, and the person in the middle will again go for one of their spots. Whoever is left out is in the middle.

In case you haven't guessed, the things you say in this game have nothing to do with who you actually like or dislike. Although it can be used to put people on the spot: "Yes, but I don't like people who still wore SpiderMan underwear in eighth grade." And then your buddy who had told you that story in secrecy is outed in front of the whole group.

The other rules of Neighbors are:
A player who moves out of his space in the circle on a turn may not return to the same space that turn.

If no one moves after someone says who they don't like, the person who said who they didn't like must go into the middle.

If only one person moves, that person is out of luck. Since he can't return to his own spot, the person who was in the middle gets it. When only one person moves, you may invoke the optional Story Rule, which simply states that when only one person moves, he or she must tell the story of the incident. Not so fun when they moved on "I don't like people wearing blue," but quite a bit of fun when they moved on "I don't like people who have accidentally walked into the wrong restroom." The Story Rule does slow the game down, so if you are playing Neighbors for the energy-building aspects of the competition for spaces in the circle, skip it.

Depending on the shyness of the players, a group can learn quite a lot about each other. I've had groups play this who have gotten into things like, "I don't like people who have had a fantasy about someone in this room," and I've had groups play this for twenty minutes talking exclusively about each other's clothes. I will warn you that seven out of ten times, someone will say something potentially inappropriate. Just keep that in mind when you decide whether or not to teach Neighbors to your Boy Scout Troop.

Focus

The facilitator is the enemy in these games. See your group come alive as they complete the ridiculously difficult tasks you assign them. The Three Pattern Game (page 27), Fake Name (page 29), Nomis Says (page 31), and Red Ball (page 28) are all games of the type that we colloquially refer to as "mindscrews." The Three-Four Rhythm (page 33) is a physical challenge that will also challenge their brains. Polish it off with Zip Zap Zop (page 35), a chance for the group to let off some steam and just play together.

Increasing the powers of concentration pays off big-time for a group. Group work requires focus on so many different levels. Whether listening to each other's ideas intently so nothing is missed, staying in character for your rehearsal when the marching band is practicing in the next room, or keeping your mind on the task at hand even though you've been working for six hours straight, the ability of a group to stay focused can help your group get a whole lot done.

7. Three Pattern Game

Players Needed: 5 to 10
Points of Concentration: Focus and concentration

LEVEL 1
Players stand in a circle. To start this game, Doug points at another person in the circle and says "you." Doug will keep his arm up so the group knows that he has gone. The person Doug pointed at will point at someone else, leaving their arm up, and say "you." This continues with each person saying "you" and pointing at someone who does not yet have their arm up. The last person to be pointed at will point at Doug.

Instruct everyone to remember who they are pointing at and then to drop their arms. They should then repeat *the same exact pattern* of pointing and saying "you." In other words, every time they say "you," they will point to the same person. We will call this pattern the "you-circle." The players should repeat the you-circle several times until they get into the groove of the pattern. Then stop.

Repeat the process used to create the you-circle by pointing at someone and keeping the arm up. However, this time instead of saying "you," each person will say the name of a different color. We will call this the "color-circle." A player may not point to the same person in the color-circle that he pointed to in the you-circle. If a player points to the same person twice, build the color-circle over again.

Again, everyone should remember who they point to in the color-circle and run through that pattern several times, until the group feels the rhythm of the color-circle. Now comes the tricky part. While continuing the color-circle, also begin the you-circle, so that you are sending two patterns around the circle at the same time.

At this point, remind the group that it is the responsibility of the player who is passing the focus to make sure that the focus is received. They can't just pass the focus without checking if the person they're passing to is paying attention. They should make eye contact and see the person respond to them before they consider the pass successful.

When the group can successfully keep both patterns going, stop them and create a third pattern. Use the category of your choice — anything from numbers to breakfast cereals. Establish the third circle on its own, then add in the color-circle and the you-circle until the group can keep all three going at once!

LEVEL 2

This is where is starts to get really hard, which when I lead these games, makes me laugh, laugh, laugh.

Play the game as above, but: instead of colors for the second round, have players say their own name. Then for the third round, players must say the name of the person they point at.

This version doesn't let players rely on sound alone; it's not enough to hear their name, they must also look to see who said it.

In both levels of this game, the common mistake is for the group to get going too fast. So slow them down when needed. It's obviously better to play this game slowly and accurately than quickly and horribly.

8. Red Ball

Players Needed: 6 or more
Points of Concentration: Focus and concentration

How many balls can you keep in the air at once? This is a great concentration and focus exercise.

Everyone stands in a circle. All of the "balls" in this game are imaginary; the players will mime them. Start by giving one player the (imaginary) red ball, and have them start to toss the red ball around the circle. When a player throws the red ball to someone else, they should make eye contact with the person they are throwing the ball to and say "red ball." The person catching the ball doesn't have to say anything until they throw it to someone else.

After everyone has gotten the hang of passing the red ball around and saying "red ball" when they throw it, toss a yellow ball into play. Obviously, when people pass the yellow ball, they should say "yellow ball." After they get into the groove of passing two balls around the circle, add a green ball.

After they've passed three balls around for a bit, freeze the action. Ask who has the red ball, the yellow ball, and the green ball. You will be amazed how often the balls change color, multiply, or disappear. If something has happened to one of the balls, reset the game so that there's one ball of each color and have them go again. If they've successfully kept track of all three balls, add a fourth.

It is the responsibility of the person throwing the ball to make sure that it is caught. If people just throw stuff around without checking if anyone is listening, that ball will be lost. This is an obvious metaphor for group communication.

Feel free to get creative with what kind of balls you toss into the circle. Some that I've used:

eight ball	ping-pong ball	beach ball
bowling ball	high ball	curve ball
bocce ball	superball	crystal ball
foul ball	debutante ball	Lucille Ball

Every time you add a ball, let them play catch for a couple minutes and then freeze the action to see if they've successfully kept track of all of them. Every time they get it right, add another one. A group is really good at this game if they can successfully keep track of a number of balls greater than half the number of people in the group.

9. The Fake Name Game

Players Needed: 6 or more
Points of Concentration: Focus and concentration

This game combines The Name Game (page 19) and The Yes Game

(page 21) with occasionally disastrous results. I love it.

LEVEL 1

Go around the circle and have every player give themself a fake name. As long as it's not their own name, it can be anything: "Jeff," "Fenderman," "Bottle," "Softly," "Zmik." It doesn't matter, as long as it's not their name and they don't mind being addressed by it.

Go through the first two levels of The Name Game (page 19). First, players pass the focus by saying their own (fake) names and pointing at the next person to speak. Then, once everyone has heard everyone's name a few times, switch so that players say the name of the person they are pointing at. Once they have the fake names down, stop them and have them rearrange the circle, shuffling up their order. Start them up again.

LEVEL 2

Stop the group and have them repeat Level 1 with a different set of fake names. You may want to have these names follow a pattern (e.g., animal nicknames like "Spider"); I like it without a pattern because it's harder.

Once the group gets to the point where they are saying the name of the person they are pointing to, stop them. Have them go back and use the first set of fake names again.

Now the kicker: Start them up using the first set of fake names. Whenever you feel like it, call "switch!" At that point, they have to switch to the second group of names and continue. Switch back and forth a couple times until they can make the switch without interrupting their rhythm.

LEVEL 3

Have the group repeat Level 1 one more time. This time, their fake name for the round is the actual first name of the person standing to their right in the circle.

Once they get that down (which could take a while), have them do the first set of names again. Then the second. Then switch among the three at will.

LEVEL 4

If they get this far, they're already focused. But sometimes, if you're like me, focused isn't good enough. In this level, start them passing around the focus using the first set of names. But this time, when someone says one of the names from another set, either by mistake or on purpose, everyone must switch to using the names of that set. One rule must be added here, that when someone switches to another set of names, that set must be used for a certain amount of time before the group can switch to a different set.

Your choice:
The easier rule is that once you switch to a new set, everyone's name must be said before you can switch again.

The harder rule is that once you switch to a new set, three names of that set must be used before you can switch again.

If desired, you can add a punishment to this game, so that, for example, if someone messes up they must only be referred to as "Bozo" until the next person messes up.

10. Nomis Says

Players Needed: Any number
Points of Concentration: Focus and concentration

The best thing about this exercise is that it's impossible to sleepwalk through. If you're not using your brain, you can't do it. It's basically an exercise in screwing with peoples' minds.

LEVEL 1
This one's not in a circle! Have the players stand spaced out around the room, so that they have some room around them to move. Try not to let anyone stand too near the wall.
The caller (you) will give instructions for people to take a step forward, back, left, or right. The players are to take a step in the *opposite* direction of the one you said. For example, if you say "back," the players are to take a step forward.
Once they've gotten the hang of this, give them three commands at a time. If you say "right, right, forward," for example, the players will have to take two steps left, then one step back.

LEVEL 2
Assign a value to the spots where people stand in the room. An

easy way to do this, if there's room, is to spread out the players in a diagonal line through the room, but have them face you. You will then be able to see everyone clearly, as you'll have a line of players facing you each one a step back and a step over from the player next to them.

The spot closest to you is "One." The object is to get to One. Play the game as above, but this time when someone follows the instructions incorrectly, they must go to the back of the line. All of the other players then move up, closer to One. If the player standing in One messes up, everybody gets to move up!

LEVEL 3

To make the game more difficult, this time you will give two directions and a number of steps to go in each direction. They must not only move in the opposite direction, but also transpose the number of steps they go in each direction. For example, if you say "go three steps right, one step forward", the correct move is one step left, then three steps back.

LEVEL 4

The grand mind-trip. You may call out single steps, multiple steps, or two numbered steps, as in Levels 1 and 3 above. This time, however, you will preface each command with either "Simon says" or "Nomis says." The commands prefaced by "Nomis says" are to be followed backwards, as above. The commands prefaced by "Simon says" are to be followed *normally*.

Examples:

Command	Proper response
Simon says, "Forward"	One step forward
Nomis says, "Right"	One step left
Nomis says, "Back, left, back"	Step forward, right, forward.
Simon says, "Right, right, left"	Step right, right, left.
Simon says, "Two steps left, one step back"	Two steps left, one step back
Nomis says, "Two steps left, one step back"	One step right, two steps forward

Continue sending players who mess up to the back of the line.

11. The Three-Four Rhythm

Players Needed: 3 or more
Points of Concentration: Focus and concentration

That's three-four as in the musical time signature, not three-fourths. This exercise is similar to the start of the kids' game Concentration, or Categories, where the group keeps a rhythm by slapping their knees, then clapping, then snapping one hand and then the other. Similar, but different. The rhythm for Categories is four-four, the most common time signature in music. (Almost all rock 'n' roll, blues, and hip-hop songs are in four-four). We are going to keep a three-four time, or "waltz time." Since you don't hear it as often, it's a little trickier.

Fig. 3

LEVEL 1:
The group stands in a circle. Everyone takes their right hand and holds it to their side, at about shoulder level, palm facing down. Then they hold their left hand at their side, at waist level, palm facing up.

Fig. 4

On the first beat, everyone will bring their right hand down and left hand up, so that they clap hands with the people to either side of them.

On the second beat, everyone will hold their hands at their sides, palms facing away from them, and again clap hands with the people to either side of them.

Fig. 5

On the third beat, everybody claps their own hands.

Fig. 6

Repeat steps one through three. It may help to have someone count out loud, either "One, two, three" or "Down, out, clap." Keep this going until everyone in the group can get in synch.

LEVEL 2:
Now that we have the clap rhythm going, it's time to sing! Pick a song *in three-four time* that everyone in the group knows, like "Take Me Out to the Ball Game" or Tom Jones' "Delilah." Then sing the song in rhythm with the clapping. The musical downbeats of the song should match up to the "down" (or "one") beats of the rhythm you're clapping.

LEVEL 3:
Once you have that down, pick another song, this time in four four time. Any song in four four that everyone knows will do fine. We always used "Help" by the Beatles or "Puttin' on the Ritz." You'll probably use some Pop song. I don't understand you kids. Anyway, try and sing along, keeping in synch with the clapping. This will be more of a

challenge, as your voice is keeping a different rhythm than your hands are. So, unlike the song you sang in Level 2 the downbeats of this song won't match up with the downbeats of the clapping.

There is usually one person in every group that plays this game that has a lot of trouble with it. The key to success is for them to not get discouraged. If they can keep their head, this game is as easy as counting to three. If someone gets really frustrated, have them build up to the clap rhythm by doing simpler movements on a three-count: for example, slap left knee, slap right knee, clap. Once they get in the rhythm, the clap rhythm should be a lot easier.

12. Zip Zap Zop

Players Needed: 5 or more
Points of Concentration: Listening, focus and concentration,
    working together

This game can be used in many different ways. The Level 1 exercise is a great way for groups to check in with one another; a way for everyone to say "Hello, we're about to work together." Its simple, repetitive nature is effective at settling the group down by helping them to forget the distractions of the rest of their lives and to give their full attention to the group.

LEVEL 1
Everyone stands in a circle. One person starts by clapping their hands, saying "zip," and pointing to someone else in the circle. The person pointed at then claps, says "zap," and points at someone else, who claps, says "zop," and points at someone else, who claps, and says "zip," and points, etcetera.

The rules of Zip Zap Zop:

1. As players pass the focus around the circle, they must say "zip, zap, zop, zip, zap, zop" in that order.
2. If someone messes up that order, the players are *not* to stop or to correct the mistaken player; rather, they are to get back into the zip zap zop pattern as quickly as possible.

LEVEL 2A

The Level 2 exercises switch the focus slightly towards working together: developing ideas and building things together as a group. The first exercise shows how a group can create without even trying.

The game is played just like Level 1, with one addition: Each person is to pass the focus in *exactly* the same way that they receive the focus. For example, if Nick claps his hands at waist level, loudly says "zzzzip," and then points to Al with his left arm straight out and his thumb and forefinger making a "gun" shape, then when Al points at someone else, he will clap at waist level, loudly say "zzzzap," and make his left hand into a gun.

People will ask you if that will get boring, since nothing will ever change. Tell them to stop questioning your almighty authority and just do the exercise. What they will discover is that the way in which the focus is passed will in fact change. The changes will happen because no two people do things exactly the same. One player may stretch out the Z sound a little more or may point the "gun" like he's shooting someone, giving the "gun" a little kick. These differences should be subconscious, but are there nonetheless.

To get these changes happening in the circle, it is sometimes necessary to remind players to pass the focus exactly as they receive it, not how they *expected* to receive it. If you think someone was intentionally changing things, ask everyone to confess if they were deliberately making changes. If someone was, do it again. Things will still change on their own, subconciously through the Group Mind.

What this shows us is that things can happen and develop in a group without one person having to push ideas forward. The changes that occur naturally are a result of the Group Mind. If everyone relaxes and trusts the Group Mind, we can develop ideas naturally and equally.

LEVEL 2B

Now that we know that things will happen on their own, we can let people get a little more involved, and get things happening faster. In Level 2B, players are allowed to make intentional changes to the way the focus is passed, within a few guidelines:

1. A change must be an *extension of* or a *reaction to* something that the group was already doing, rather than a non sequitur. For example:

   If people are giggling when they pass they focus,

someone could laugh uproariously like Falstaff, or evilly like a James Bond villain, as an extension of the giggles. If people are passing the focus very loudly, someone could whisper, in reaction to the yelling.

2. A change cannot be made until the collective group has adjusted to the previous change made.

3. A change should be made because it is needed by the group, not because someone has a funny idea. A change is needed by the group when everyone has adjusted to the previous change and is no longer particularly inspired by it.

Players should be instructed to follow the changes wherever they lead. They may stop saying "zip, zap, zop," or making any noise at all. Or, they might start saying whole sentences, instead of nonsense words.

By giving players the ability to change things, the group should be able to create a constantly evolving pattern, that never gets boring or repetitive, where everyone in the circle is an equal part of the process. Note that people who support new ideas are just as important as the people who introduce new ideas. After all, if I start to whisper, it doesn't help the group until someone else affirms my move by also whispering.

LEVEL 2C

This is totally optional, but sometimes fun things can happen if you repeat the exercise, reminding the group that while following the changes, they also don't have to stay in a circle as long as they can keep an awareness of what everyone is doing. This exercise has occasionally led to Follow-the-Leader style games that go around the room, outside, into nearby stores, etc. Please watch out for traffic.

Awareness

These games train you to see with the eyes in the back of your head. You will develop a sixth sense about your teammates, so that you will know where they are and what they are doing at all times. Even when they go home at night. If one of you gets hurt, the others will feel the pain. I may be exaggerating a bit. But these games are great for getting people to stop thinking about themselves all of the time and to give their attention to their teammates.

Start your group off with Sound Ball (page 38), one of my favorite games, which is fun and noisy and also teaches your group the joy of building on someone else's idea versus simply generating your own. After that, Killer (page 42), Find the Leader (page 41), and the most advanced Clap Pass (page 39) will make them practice looking at everyone in the group simultaneously. When they've got that down, you're ready to move on to the next level, One to Twenty (page 43) and Scream Circle (page 44), which require them to *sense* everyone in the group simultaneously.

13. Sound Ball

Players Needed: 5 or more
Points of Concentration: Group awareness, listening and support, energy building, focus and concentration

LEVEL 1
Players stand in a circle. Doug begins by passing an imaginary "ball" to Karen. As he passes the ball, Doug makes a sound — any sound. When Karen catches the ball, she makes the same sound. Then Karen passes the ball to someone else, making a different sound. The person who catches Karen's ball makes Karen's sound, then passes with his own sound, and so on.

The best thing about this game is that it forces people to listen. Before someone can pass the ball, they must respond to the person who gave them the ball. If people are not listening, but are instead thinking about what noise they're going to use next time, they will not be able to respond properly. This dynamic has a parallel in group discussions or arguments: people should listen to the points that others are making before coming in with their own.

It also has a parallel in improvisation: Improvised scenework has the rule of "yes, and." I agree to your idea, and then build upon it with my own. Repeating the thrower's noise as you catch the Sound Ball is the equivalent of the "yes." Throwing with your own noise is the "and."

Be very tough with people who try to pass the ball without repeating the passer's noise first.

LEVEL 2

Once people have the general idea, you can make this game a ton of fun by first speeding it up as fast as you can go, and then starting a second and possibly third Sound Ball going around. You have not lived until you've seen a group of ten people all screaming ridiculous noises as they pass pretend balls back and forth.

14. Clap Pass

Players Needed: 5 or more
Points of Concentration: Group awareness, focus and concentration,
    energy building

LEVEL 1

Players stand in a circle. Doug starts by making eye contact with the person on his right. Those two people simultaneously clap their hands. The second player then turns to the player on her other side and makes eye contact. Then those two people simultaneously clap. Continue around the circle, each person clapping simultaneously with first the person to their left, then their right. In this manner, the clap will travel around the circle. See how fast you can go! When the claps stop happening simultaneously, slow down until you're back on track, then speed up again.

LEVEL 2

In this level, play as in Level 1, but anytime someone chooses to, they can reverse direction and send the clap back the way it came instead of passing it on. This is done by maintaining eye contact with the person with whom you just clapped, instead of turning to the person next to you, and clapping together for a second time.

LEVEL 3

This level is pretty tough. In this level, you no longer have to go right around the circle. Pass the clap to anyone you make eye contact with. To reinforce the importance of that last sentence, say it out loud to whoever is closest to you right now. Anyhow, as with the above levels, get going as fast as you can, slowing down when necessary to hold the ship together.

The key to this game is eye contact. If you don't make eye contact with someone, it is impossible to clap simultaneously with them. When the group gets going with this game, they will establish a rhythm. The rhythm is a good thing, but it is more important to have the claps occur simultaneously than to maintain the rhythm. So, if you are about to pass to someone and you notice that they aren't looking at you or aren't ready, you need to hold back your clap until the other person is ready to clap with you.

When you are not the one clapping, it's your job to try to make eye contact with whoever has the clap at any given moment. This way, if they decide to pass to you, you'll be ready to receive it.

15. Group Mirror

Players Needed: 3 or more
Points of Concentration: Group awareness, focus and concentration

Players start in a circle. Everyone notes the person on their right. Then, players spread out all over the room. They can stand anywhere, as long as they can see the person who was formerly on their right in the circle. They will be watching this person only during this exercise.

Once everyone has a clear view of the person they need to watch, they will mirror that person: match the way they're standing and match any motion that they do. Eventually, everyone will be standing the same way and doing the same things.

At first, instruct the group that no one is to intentionally start any motions; the only moves they should make are moves that they see their watch-ee do. This should have the effect of sending individuals' mannerisms around the circle. For instance, if someone habitually giggles or bites their lip, the giggle or bite will travel around the circle. Once a movement starts, it should never stop, unless it changes to something else. If a movement stops, someone has dropped it.

Next take turns having people lead the group in motion. Leaders are still responsible for mirroring what they see. Ideally, the group will undergo a series of smooth transitions from one motion to the next.

This exercise is a good, simple way to demonstrate the Group Mind.

Even when no one initiates a movement, there will still be motion happening around the circle. This idea, that action is happening even when no one individual in the group is adding anything, is what the Group Mind is all about.

16. Find the Leader

Players Needed: 7 or more.
Other Needs: An area where one person can go and not be able
     to see or hear the rest of the group (in other words, a room
     that someone can leave)
Points of Concentration: Group awareness, focus and concentration

Doug leaves the room. The rest of the group decides which one of them will be the leader for the round. The group then sits or stands in a circle and begins a simple, repetitive motion initiated by the leader. Doug is then called back in, and he stands in the center of the circle.

The group's job is to do whatever the leader does. The leader's job is to transform or change the action that people do without being obvious. Doug's job is to identify the leader.

Two things that can make the leader very easy to identify are 1) if the leader makes big huge changes that are tough to miss (Hmm. Karen was the first one to sit down, so I'll guess it's her!) or 2) if everyone in the group is looking at the leader. For this reason, it is helpful to play the game like Group Mirror, where everyone looks at a different person in the circle (e.g., the person to their right) and follows them. Eventually someone will be following the leader.

The Doug in the middle has three guesses as to who the leader is. If he guesses right, he chooses who leaves the room next. If he doesn't guess right in three tries, the leader for that round chooses who leaves the room next. And yes, he can send the same person back out again.

This game is one of those where you can trick people into learning stuff while they're playing a fun game. The person in the middle is training their observation skills. The others get practice in thinking as one group instead of many individuals. The ideal goal for the circle is for each person to successfully anticipate the leader's next move, so that the transformations are seamless. If everyone is able to switch a motion at the same time to the same thing, it will be impossible for the person in the middle to find the leader.

17. Killer

Players Needed: At least 6; the more the better
Other Needs: A deck of cards, or several scraps of paper,
     one per player
Points of Concentration: Group awareness, group bonding

To begin, count out one playing card or one scrap of paper per person. Make sure the Queen of Spades is one of the cards in your pile, or make an X on one of the pieces of paper. Distribute the cards or papers among all of the players, telling them to look at their card but not to let anyone else see it.

The person who gets the Queen of Spades or the X is the killer for this round. The killer's goal is to "kill" everyone. Everyone else's goal is to identify the killer first.

The killer "kills" people by making eye contact and winking at them. If someone is winked at, they must count to themselves to three and then die as theatrical a death as possible. Seriously, go big. There is no such concept as "over the top" when it comes to your death scene.

The killer should, of course, try to wink at people when no one else is looking. Everyone else needs to try to keep an eye on everyone else's eyes, while not getting winked at themselves. A player may try to catch the killer at any time by simply saying their name: "It's Dan." If they're right, the round is over. If they're wrong, they're out and must die a suitably humble and apologetic death.

If you have a large group, multiple killers may be used. If one killer kills another killer, the murdered killer must make a deathbed confession and hopefully atone for their wicked ways as a part of their death scene.

When all killers are identified or the last innocent is killed, the round is over. Reshuffle the cards and start again.

This game provides a great challenge: observe everybody else, all the time. It's the same goal for the killers and innocents — the innocents have to try to catch the killer winking at someone (else), the killer needs to make sure the coast is clear before striking. It's a great tool to get people to start considering themselves part of a larger group, instead of just one solo individual.

18. One to Twenty

Players Needed: 5 or more
Points of Concentration: Group awareness, focus and
    concentration, listening

This is one of the greatest group exercises of all time. This game forces people to think as a member of a group, not as an individual. Thinking selfishly prevents the group from reaching the goal.

The group stands in a circle. The group must count from one to twenty. If more than one person says a number at the same time, the group must start over again at zero. The group may not follow any preset order: They can't take turns by going right around the circle, they can't have one person say all the even numbers. In fact, any strategy discussion among the group at all is forbidden.

If the group makes it to twenty right away, have them do it again. Once they have to start over twice, it will take them at least five more tries to get it right. If they have a lot of trouble, have them vary their speed: first try it really fast, then really slow. Slow is easier. Once they are successful, have them do it again with their eyes closed and/or with their backs toward the center of the circle. Some people find it easier with eyes closed, some harder.

Although no discussion is allowed of how to achieve the task, a group may come up with a system on its own. For instance, Doug may say "one" while staring or pointing at Karen, indicating to the group that Karen will say "two" and indicate who will say "three." As long as no one says out loud what is happening; that is, as long as everyone in the group notices the system on their own and agrees to themselves to follow it, any method the group comes up with is great! First of all, the group has worked together to solve the problem. While one person may initiate the system, no one can instruct the group as to how the system works. So no one can elevate themselves into a leadership role. The group must truly work as a team of equals. Second, whatever system they come up with probably won't work when you make them close their eyes.

If the group uses a system of rules, such as pointing at the next person to speak or stomping before saying the next number (a popular "eyes closed" system), make them do it once without a net. No clever indications, just paying attention to the group.

Some hints:

Take your time. If you rush, others will also rush, and eventually you'll rush into each other. Don't think ahead, think in the now. If you decide that you are going to say fifteen, then all that you're paying attention to is whoever says fourteen. So you won't notice the guy next to you who has also started to say fifteen. Instead, think to yourself, "Does the group need me to say this number?" If the answer is yes, then say it.

Once this task is done successfully, and you ask them how they did it, you will usually get the answer. "We just settled into a rhythm." This rhythm is the Group Mind at work. You will notice that once they find the rhythm, they will usually begin to sense whether someone else is going to say a number. They will tune in to each other so completely that they can basically read each other's intentions. It is a very cool game to watch.

19. Scream Circle

Players Needed: An even number of players, 6 or more
Points of Concentration: Group awareness, focus and
     concentration, energy building, group bonding

This game is silly. Players get in a close circle with their arms around the shoulders of the person to either side of them. They need to find the person directly across the circle from them, the person to their left, and the person to their right.

Everyone puts their heads down, looking at the floor. Someone will then count "one, two, three." On three, everyone will look up at one of those three people — the person to the left, right, or across from them. If the person they look at is looking back at them, both players scream. Then everyone puts their head down, and the process is repeated. Keep going until when you look up, no one screams.

If you have an odd number of players, you can have people rotate out of the circle to be the counter.

This game works best with a group of eight to twelve. With six players, it will probably be a short game; with more than twelve it can get long. If the group chances to hit upon a "no scream" arrangement in the first three to five tries, just have them start over; the second one will take longer. Long games of Scream Circle are OK. When the silence finally hits, so much tension has built up that the silence seems louder than the screams.

The group really feels like they've accomplished something. It's a very bonding game.

Creation

These games are great for use at the beginning or end of your session. They're the equivalent of taking the leash off of your dog and letting him run around the park. When I use them in my improv classes, the best thing about them is that they allow the players to get some laughs. Getting that sort of positive reinforcement works for me in two ways: it gets the players enthusiastic to continue, so they can get more laughs; also, it relaxes them, as they no longer have to worry about when their first laugh is going to come. They can now focus on more challenging exercises, that maybe have less immediate gratification.

Although these games allow players to get laughs and be clever, it is important to notice that every laugh someone can get in one of these exercises is built off of an idea of one of their teammates. So the focus remains on teamwork, not individual accomplishment. These games illustrate the marriage between using the ideas of your comrades and running free with your own.

20. Object Pass

Players Needed: Any number
Points of Concentration: Group creation

In this game we pretend that we are working with some magical Silly Putty. This is Silly Putty that does not have to obey the Law of Conservation of Energy — it can become whatever size, thickness, or complexity you want.

The group stands in a circle. Doug starts by taking a ball of the imaginary putty, shaping it into an object, and using the object. The object can be anything at all as long as it is recognizable when it is used. For example, Doug shapes the putty into an umbrella. When he opens it and puts it over his head, it is clear to everyone that he's got an umbrella.

Once he has used the object, he passes it to someone around the circle. Oh, let's say, Karen. Karen must take the object, use the object, and then reshape the putty into a new object.

Karen takes the umbrella and puts it over her shoulder. Sticking out her palm, she realizes that it's not raining and closes the umbrella, now resting on it like a cane. She picks up the putty umbrella and smooshes the closed cover into the stem of the umbrella, making a long cylinder of putty. She then squeezes the cylinder to make it more narrow all the way down. Finally, she turns the bottom end to the side and smashes it flat, so that she now has a putty golf club. After swinging the golf club, everybody knows what it is. She passes the club to someone else, who uses it, then reshapes it, and so on.

Again, the putty is *magic* putty, so it can shrink to make a marble or expand to make a car. The fun of this game is in the process of reshaping the putty. Ideally, the object made won't be too far removed from the object received, or the game will go on forever. Players should be encouraged to choose their next object based on the object they receive. The connection between objects can be based on either *appearance* (When I close this umbrella, it is long and skinny. What else is long and skinny? A golf club.) or *association* (I used the golf club to hit a ball, now I have to go find the ball, so I'll reshape this golf club into a golf cart and drive after it). The fun of the game is to see the connections from object to object. After all, anybody could walk in off the street with an idea about shaping the putty into a guitar. Making a guitar because you thought of a guitar that morning is not as impressive as making a guitar because you were handed a tennis racket.

As in Sound Ball (page 38), it is important that each player use the object received before reshaping it. Using the object received does two important things. First, it enforces the idea that you must acknowledge every gift that you receive. Second, it gives a player a chance to build on the ideas of the previous player by using their object in a different way. A chair can be used to reach a high shelf. A golf club can be broken over the knee in frustration. An umbrella can be used to kill Batman. These opportunities to be supportive while being creative are the heart of this exercise.

21. Yes And

Players Needed: 2 or more
Points of Concentration: Listening, group creation

In this exercise two players at a time build a scene together. The scene may not look particularly realistic, because the scene will be built very slowly and in a way that the two players each contribute exactly half of the scene.

Give the players a suggestion of a location for the scene to take place. Doug will start the scene by saying anything at all that he might say in the given location.

Karen will then literally "Yes And" Doug's first line; that is, she will repeat the information that Doug gave to the scene in his line, then say "and," and then add new information to the scene, building on Doug's line. Make sure that the two thoughts are connected with "and" and not "but" or "or." "But" implies that there is a problem with the last contribution to the scene, and we want to accept everything. "Or" is a way of saying, "I heard your idea, but mine is better," which is strictly taboo in this exercise.

Here is an example on the suggestion of "laundromat."

DOUG: "This load is ready for the dryer."

KAREN: "That load is ready for the dryer and I need to get change for a dollar."

DOUG: "You need to get change for a dollar, and I have it because I always think ahead."

KAREN: "You always think ahead and you never pass up a chance to remind me of that."

DOUG: "I always remind you of that and it frustrates me that you still don't think ahead."

KAREN: "It frustrates you that I don't think ahead and I need to borrow some of your fabric softener."

Here are several reasons why Doug and Karen did this exercise so brilliantly. And believe me, this example was brilliant:

First, they kept using "and" and moving forward, even when feeling negative emotions. If in the second-to-last line, Doug had instead said "I always remind you of that but you never do it," the scene would have become an argument.

Second, they made the scene interesting by making it about their relationship. (This is most important when using this game as a theater exercise. As a group-building exercise, it's not vital to the success of the exercise, but it does make it a lot more interesting to watch.) After the first three lines, this scene could have become a discussion about quarters: who gets them, when, and why. But by talking about how they feel about each other, Doug and Karen make the scene about two people trying to irritate each other.

Third, it is possible for Doug and Karen to make the scene about their relationship because they successfully keep the scene in the present. That is, they don't talk about things they did in the past or will do in the future. Everything they talked about was happening right in the moment. As a result of this, we can take Karen's last line as an intentional jab: "Your reminders that I don't plan ahead irritate me, so I am going to put another example of my unpreparedness in your face because I know it frustrates you."

You can edit the scenes after a minute or so by simply calling "scene." When the exercise is done well, the dialog may not sound realistic, but the relationship between the characters in the scene should seem realistic. Also, each player will have contributed equally to the scene. They built it together by building on top of each other's ideas. Which, obviously, is the point of the exercise. It shows the players how to collaborate selflessly. For the exercise to be successful, each player must treat the other's ideas as equally if not more important than their own.

22. Art Gallery

Players Needed: 4 or more
Points of Concentration: Creativity, quick thinking, support

Fig. 7a   Fig. 7b

This is a good blow off-steam game, because it is fast-paced and rewards creativity. There's usually a lot of laughs in this game. I normally use it after a bunch of more cerebral games like Red Ball (page 28) or The Fake Name Game (page 29).

48

Players stand in a back line or a circle — whatever makes it easiest for them to see everybody else. Doug starts by going into the playing area and striking some sort of pose. Karen then enters and adds on to Doug's pose. Karen can add on in any way she sees fit (see Fig. 7a and 7b) — she doesn't necessarily have to touch Doug, mirror Doug, etc. She just has to somehow respond to Doug.

Once Doug and Karen are frozen in their poses, a third player also joins the tableau. These three people are now a work of art. It is up to one of the remaining players to name this work of art. As quickly as possible, one of the players in the line or circle will state the title of this piece of art.

Fig. 8 The Mummy's Curse

The title should be inspired by the poses of the "artwork" players, but doesn't need to make sense to anybody but the person giving the title. Figures 8 and 9 are examples of some tableaus and some possible titles. As you can see, they don't really need to make sense. Once the title is given, the stage is cleared and the player who gave the title starts the next tableau.

Fig. 9 An Interesting School Day

As the game progresses, you can relax the rules: you can have more or fewer than three people in the tableau, you can allow the tableau to move, you can give a piece of art multiple titles. Have fun with it; see how you can play around with the form of the game. After all, the art world is ever evolving.

The most fun element of this game is the quick-draw titles. As soon as the group realizes that you can get a laugh with a particularly clever title, they will try really hard to come up with the best title possible. The fast pace of the game, and the fact that you only have a couple seconds to come up with a title, will get players to bypass their normal self-editors and give them direct access to the instinctive, creative part of their brains. Also, you will see people get less and less self-conscious about their posing as the artwork. Players realize that the more committed and contorted the art, the more interesting a title can be conceived. So instead of being worried about whether they look silly, players will actually try to look sillier in order to help each other out!

23. Freeze Tag (aka Freeze, aka Switch)

Players Needed: 4 or more
Points of Concentration: Creation, support

If you have ever seen improvisation in your life, then you probably don't need me to explain how this game works. This is the Adam and Eve of improvisation. Actually, God probably invented Freeze first, then invented people to play it. The day a caveman first picked up a rock to use as a hammer, another caveman yelled "freeze!" and started using it as a bowling ball.

Anyway, if you're unfamiliar with the game, here's how it's played. If you already know the basics, skip down to where we talk about how to play it well.

Everyone stands in a back line except for the first two players. These two players improvise a scene. During the scene, any player in the back line can call out "Freeze!" That player will then come forward and tag out one of the players in the scene. Let's say Karen tags out Doug. Doug returns to the back line. Karen takes the *exact physical position* that Doug was in when she froze the scene. Karen then begins a new scene that is based on the positions that she and the other player are now in.

Fig. 10

Example:
Doug and Paul are astronauts. Doug plants a flag on the moon. Karen shouts, "Freeze!"

Karen tags out Doug and takes his flag-planting pose. She then initiates the new scene by saying "We've got a lot of butter to churn for the barn-raising, Hezekiah!"

Fig. 11

Karen took the hand position of planting a flag and transformed it into that of churning butter. Karen and Paul now continue their Amish scene until someone else freezes them.

It doesn't matter which player you tag out; the next person to tag in doesn't have to tag out Paul since Doug was tagged out last time. Tag out whoever you want.

Each new scene should be unrelated to the previous scene. You are not tagging in to take over and continue a scene; you are starting a brand new scene each time.

OK, those of you who skipped the description can rejoin the group now. I hope you enjoyed your break.

Obviously, the most entertaining part of this game is coming up with the fun ideas. However, some people are better than others at seeing possible transformations. Even worse, some people have stock Freeze Tag bits (see sidebar). For these reasons, you should encourage the players not to wait until they have an idea to call "freeze." On the contrary, they should call "freeze" when the scene needs to be edited.

When Freeze Tag is played poorly, it is usually because the players consider it a game of Creation, forgetting that it is also a game of Support. The truth is, the players in the back line are just as important to the

The Freeze Tag Hall of Fame

There are people out there who have their three favorite Freeze Tag bits and will not call "Freeze" unless one of them appears. This is not imaginative and not fun. Get your group to be surprising and creative! Here are a few bits in the "Freeze Tag Hall of Fame." I've seen each of these bits at least fifty times over my improv career. Challenge yourself and your group to come up with scenes more imaginative than:

- Siamese twins
- The "You Must Be Taller Than This Sign to Get on the Ride" sign
- Tattoo, from *Fantasy Island*, seeing a plane
- Someone walking in on a couple in a compromising position
- "Rock, Paper, Scissors" and
- Anything super-glued to anything else

success of the scene on-stage as the players who are performing it. At least three-fourths of unsuccessful Freeze Tag scenes fail because they are edited too early or too late.

This situation makes me crazy when I watch this game: Someone calls freeze and enters a scene. They say their opening line of dialog. The other person in the scene starts to respond but only gets two words out before someone else in the back line yells "Freeze!" The person in the back line yelled "Freeze" because they had a funny idea based on the players positions, and he wants to get his joke out before the players move and the position is gone. This player was so intent on getting his own idea out that he neglected to listen to the scene that was actually on-stage. When this happens, the interrupter and the person interrupted both look like idiots.

Another frequent problem with this game is when a scene goes on and on forever. Usually in this case, no one edits the scene because they don't have an idea yet. This causes the whole game to be dragged down.

Both of these problems have the same solution: Call "freeze" when the scene is over. That could be after one line or it could be after four minutes. But pay attention to the scene. Then support the scene by giving it a nice finishing point. You have now made your fellow players look as good as possible. Good job!

A side effect of this process is that you yourself will look better. I guarantee you that in the five seconds between saying "freeze" and taking that position, you will come up with something to say. It doesn't have to be clever, as you have a scene partner out there who can build on your idea. It is much more impressive to see the two of you create something on the spot together than to watch someone come out and say their preconceived idea.

This is a great game to play at the end of a class or workshop, as it allows the players a lot of freedom to just get out there and play around. It's fun.

If you have players who are hesitant about getting into the scenes, or if you have players that dominate the game, or if editing is a problem, I recommend the Blind Freeze (page 53) variation of this game.

24. Blind Freeze

Players Needed: 4 or more
Points of Concentration: Creation, quick thinking, support

This game basically works just like Freeze Tag (page 50). Two players do a scene, another player tags in and starts a new scene based on the positions. But Blind Freeze gives it a twist.

The players still stand in a back line. However, the player at the far right end of the line turns their back to the stage so that they can't see the positions of the players. The player at the far left end of the line is responsible for calling "freeze." When the player at the left calls "freeze," the player at the right must turn around and tag into the scene. The player tagged out goes to the left end of the line.

I love this version of Freeze, as it isolates the elements of the game, which makes them easier to work on. The player on the left only has to worry about editing the scene. He doesn't have to worry about whether he has an idea, because he's not the one that has to enter the scene. So he can focus entirely on picking an editing point which gives the scene a nice satisfying finish. The player on the right can't pre-plan an idea, because she doesn't know what the positions of the players are. She will impress herself when she quickly enters the scene and comes up with something great.

25. Layers

Players Needed: 5 to 9
Points of Concentration: Creation, focus and concentration,
    give and take, group awareness

This game combines elements of Freeze Tag (page 50) with a memory game. Due to the memory aspects of the game, the bigger your group, the harder the game. For this reason I wouldn't go any higher than nine people. If you have ten, break them up into two groups of five and do the exercise twice.

If you have five to seven people in the group, start with one person on-stage. If you have eight or nine, start with two. Give your starting players a suggestion. They will begin a scene based on the suggestion. (If you start with one person, make sure it's a scene and not a monolog — the difference is that people giving a monolog just stand there, while people in a scene have an environment around them, so they have activities to do.)

Let's assume we have a group of five. The first player starts a scene based on the suggestion. At some point, one of the off-stage players will call "freeze," and the player in the scene will freeze. The off-stage player will then add on — not tag out — and start a new scene, incorporating the position. So it is now a two-person scene. Eventually a third player will freeze the scene, enter, and begin a three-person scene based on the positions of the first two players. The pattern continues, with the group doing a four- and then five-person scene.

At this point the group has done five unrelated scenes. They will now go back down to a one-person scene. The players who entered the scene will now exit in reverse order. So the player who entered to create the five-person scene will find a reason to leave the scene. As soon as this player is gone, the four remaining players must revert to the *same four-person scene* they did before, picking up where they left off. The fourth player in will find a reason to leave, and the remaining players will return to the three-person scene, then to the two-person scene, and finally back to the one-person scene we started with.

The part of this game that is the most fun is building a scene based on a whole bunch of people out on-stage. It is a good opportunity for players to just be creative and have fun. The game then gets tricky as the players have to remember everything they did in order to get back to the beginning. In addition, the big-group scenes give an opportunity to explore give and take, as the scenes won't be successful if everyone is shouting over each other. Players must figure out who in the larger scenes should have the focus, and generously give it to them. The final pitfall of this game is that players must pay attention to when someone enters or leaves a scene, or they will suddenly find themselves the only one left in the garden while everybody else has moved on to the museum.

Energy

Get that blood pumping. Physiologically speaking, physical activity increases circulation and, therefore, blood flow to the brain, stimulating thought. Practically speaking, getting people moving with an exercise that is loud and/or fun is a very good way to get them excited to do whatever comes up next. Sometimes, you just need to run around like a kid for a while to shake off the baggage from the rest of the day or to help you wake up. These exercises range from very simple to complex. Little Red Wagon (page 55) is just yelling; Eights (page 56) is basically jumping around. Some of the games get more complex, but they all share a goal: to get everybody running around, pumped up, and playful. These games should be unadulterated — and un-adult — fun.

26. Little Red Wagon

Players Needed: Any number
Point of Concentration: Energy building

This is a really simple bit I learned at camp. I use it on those gray days where everyone is acting like they're half asleep and their clothes are too heavy.

It's an easy little verse, which will be repeated ten times:

You can't ride my little red wagon.
The wheels are busted and the axle's draggin'.
Chug, chug.
(Second) verse
A little bit louder and a little bit worse.

Obviously, you'll change the "second" to whatever verse comes next. In verse number nine, I usually have them say "last" instead of "tenth." And I end the tenth verse after "chug, chug."

The idea here is that the first verse will be whispered, and the tenth verse will be screamed at the top of their lungs. In between, each verse should get, as the poet said, "a little bit louder." You may need to caution your players to start pretty quietly and to take their time with the volume-building, so they still have somewhere to go when they reach ten. If your players are already screaming as loud as they can by eight, and then they still have to get louder twice, vocal strain may result. Yeah, your musical group might not want to use this one.

But for the rest of you, you will be amazed at how much laziness and/or sleepiness can be conquered with just a little screaming.

27. Eights

Players Needed: Any number
Points of Concentration: Energy building, working together

This is another really easy warm-up. Sometimes a nice physical warm-up is all that's needed to get your mind warmed up. And this will do that. It's basically a fast, grown-up Hokey Pokey.

Everyone stands in a circle and begins by shaking their right hand into the circle eight times, counting out loud to eight as they do it. It is important that everyone stay together, as this will help get the group into the groove of working together. Then they shake the left hand into the circle eight times, then the right foot, then the left foot, counting out loud to eight each time.

Immediately after that, start over with the right hand, this time only counting to seven. Do seven shakes of right hand, left hand, right foot, left foot. Repeat the cycle six more times, counting out loud every shake, going up to six, then five, four, three, two, one.

ALTERNATE METHOD:
I don't know what difference it makes, but you can also start with sixteen shakes and do half as many each time: sixteen, eight, four, two, one.

Either way, the "One! One! One! One!" round is kind of fun.

28. What Are You Doing?

Players Needed: 3 or more
Points of Concentration: Energy building, quick thinking,
    focus and concentration

This is an old classic. It can be played as a relay game or a round robin. Two players will start on-stage; the others should either form one line behind the playing area or two lines to either side of the playing area.

LEVEL 1

Doug starts doing a physical activity. Let's say he's doing jumping jacks. Karen asks Doug, "What are you doing?" Doug can say he's doing anything *except* what he's actually doing: In this example, Doug can't say he's doing jumping jacks. So he says, "I'm kicking the tires on an old car."

At this point, Karen must do the activity that Doug just described. (Actually, she will mime that activity. She doesn't need to go outside and find an old car.) Once Karen has taken on the activity described by Doug, now Doug will ask Karen "What are you doing?" and Karen will have to name an activity that's not the one she's actually doing. Then Doug will take on that activity, and so on.

This is an elimination game. A player is eliminated if he:

- Says he is doing the activity he is really doing;
- Hesitates too long before answering the question;
- Re-uses any part of an activity previously used. For instance in the above example, Karen would be out if she said she were kicking a dog, inflating a tire, or driving a car, because kicking, tires, and cars were already used.

When a player is eliminated, he or she goes to the end of the back line (if the others are in one line) or the end of the line on his or her side of the stage (if they're in two lines).

LEVEL 2

If the group is a little too good at this, you can add a degree of difficulty by choosing two letters. Then, every activity someone says they're doing must include words that start with those letters.

Example:

Letters G, B

Legal: **G**rabbing **B**ooks, **G**etting **B**y, **G**oing for **B**roke, **G**esturing **B**roadly, **G**rating **B**rie, **G**olfing on the **B**us

Illegal: Going Nuts (No B); Blowing Gas (wrong order); GumBalls (only one word)

Then use three letters, then four. Remember, you still can't repeat words; once someone uses "going," no one else can!

The more fast-paced this game is played, the better. The speed of the game gets the mind working fast, and all of the mime-action gets your body moving, so this is a great all-around energy exercise.

29. Category Tag

Players Needed: 5 or more
Point of Concentration: Energy building, fun

Yes, this is Tag, like on the playground. Before you say, "My group is a group of grown adults; there is no way they are ever going to play tag," let me tell you that you have not seen fun until you have seen a group of grown-ups playing tag. The moment when a forty-year-old man's attitude changes from "This is stupid, making us play tag like a bunch of kids" to "You're going down, Jennings! Prepare to be It!" is the closest thing to real magic that I have ever personally witnessed. So unless there's an imminent risk of heart attack, I recommend tag.

Now, to jazz it up, I recommend Category Tag, which is a more generalized version of TV Tag. In TV Tag, a player who is not It can freeze and call out the name of a TV show. They are then safe from being tagged until they move again. However, if a player calls out the name of a TV Show that has already been called out by another player, then they automatically become It. Beyond that, it's normal Tag — one player is It, and if It tags another player, that player becomes It. You can decide for your group whether to allow tagbacks.

Category Tag is the same as TV Tag, except you can make the category of "safe phrases" (which in TV Tag is "TV shows") anything you want. It can be as general as TV shows or as specific as "Mel Gibson movies." It can be specific to your group, such as "products our company makes" or "one of your lines from the play."

Since you have control over the category, you have control over the secondary purpose of the game. You can use it to reinforce the points of an earlier meeting. ("You're safe if you say one of the goals of our fall promotion"). You can use it to get people thinking freely ("You're safe if you give a synonym of 'success'") or laughing ("You're safe if you give a synonym of 'passing gas'." That one probably won't work for every group.) Or make them feel a little rebellious, or to vent ("You're safe when you say something that bugs you about _____"). One of the groups I perform with made it so that you were safe if you did an imitation of me. The best thing about Category Tag is that you can get people to learn or remember things while they're running around like little kids.

30. Emotional Volume

Players Needed: Any number
Points of Concentration: Energy building, acting preparation

This exercise is specifically designed for theater groups. It should work equally well for improvisers and actors, in class or before a show. It's basically a warm-up lap through the range of emotions.

Players spread out across the room giving themselves their own space to work in. Tell them to imagine a volume knob on their emotions, going from zero to ten. Zero is neutrality, one is very subtle emotion, and ten is intense emotion. Start by giving them an emotion like "angry" and a low level like two. Let everyone find their own way to express the emotion. Then, start fiddling with the volume knob, turning it up and down. As numbers go higher, the players must embody stronger and stronger emotions. If the emotion was "angry," for instance, at level 2 the players would show mild irritation, while at ten they would be in a blinding rage.

Give them a range of emotions both negative, like anger or sorrow, and positive, like happiness and hope. Let them explore the range of intensity within each emotion. And, of course, end up with one of the dials going to eleven.

I created this exercise after noticing that a lot of students in my Sunday-at-noon improv class had trouble getting into character and acting with emotion. They were still getting started with their day, and so they were hesitant to dive into intense emotion. By using this exercise to warm them up, and force them to display extreme emotional states, it was easier for them later on in the class to show the comparatively lesser amounts of emotion that their scenes required. Another good name for this exercise would be Emotional Scales. It just takes them through their emotions once so that the territory is comfortable when they get there for real.

31. Kitty Wants a Corner

Players Needed: 7 or more; you can get away with 6.
Points of Concentration: Energy building, group awareness

This game is Duck Duck Goose for grown-ups. One person gets in the middle of the circle. That person is the kitty. The kitty goes to someone on the outside of the circle and says, "Kitty wants a corner."

The person on the outside of the circle will reply, "See my neighbor," and will point in the direction of the neighbor he wants the kitty to see. The kitty will go in the direction pointed (but does not necessarily have to go to the very next person) and again ask, "Kitty wants a corner." And so on.

While all of that is going on, it is everyone else's job to try to switch places in the circle with another person on the outside of the circle as often as possible. In order to do this, a pair of potential place-switchers will need to first establish eye contact, so that they can signal each other to go. They don't want to signal each other vocally, because every time people try to switch places, the kitty will try to get into one of the open spaces, leaving whoever doesn't get a spot to become the new kitty.

It is legal but lame to switch places with the person next to you. The more daring you are and the closer you can come to switching places with the person directly across the circle from you, the cooler you are.

Everyone has a lot of fun with this game. It is important, however, for everyone's safety that you frequently remind the circle to step back and stay wide. As the game progresses, people have a tendency to creep in closer to each other. So back them up every so often so they don't kill each other.

32. Get Down!

Players Needed: 3 or more
Points of Concentration: Energy building, working together

I am told that this game is actually used by cheerleaders as a warm-up. Everyone stands in a circle and starts clapping in rhythm. Doug starts by picking someone by calling their name. Then, the group follows this script (I also indicated where the claps should fall):

DOUG: Hey Don! (clap)
DON: Hey what? (clap)
EVERYONE BUT DON: Hey Don! (clap)
DON: Hey what? (clap)
EVERYONE BUT DON: Show us how (clap) to get down!
DON: No way! (clap)
EVERYONE BUT DON: Show us how (clap) to get down!
DON: OK!
EVERYONE: D, O, W, N. That's the way to get down! Uh huh!

D, O, W, N, that's the way to get down!

During the first "D, O, W, N. That's the way to get down," Don will, in fact, get down, dancing to the beat. Don can do any dance he wants to, but it should be something the other group can follow. Because, on the second "D, O, W, N ..." line, the entire group will do the dance that Don just showed them.

Then, Don gets to pick the lucky person to go next.

DON: Hey Mary!
MARY: Hey what?
EVERYONE BUT MARY: Hey Mary!
MARY: Hey what?

... And so on. After everyone has had a chance to lead the group in their funky dance, the last person to get down will start the next verse with;

LAST GUY: Hey everyone!
EVERYONE: Hey what?
EVERYONE: Hey everyone!
EVERYONE: Hey what?

Well, actually, everyone says every line. When you get to "D, O, W, N ...," each person does the dance that they introduced to the group. Then do a split kick and form a pyramid! Just kidding. Split kicks are optional.

Dynamics

Remember before when I said that these exercises force the group to work as one, with no individual ever taking the wheel? Well, I lied a little bit. The exercises in this chapter actually require individuals to step up and drive for a while, to carry the group forward. But here's the important thing: they also require those individuals to relinquish control back to the group.

In theory, group projects can be accomplished purely as a group. Also in theory, a communist society is viable. But the Soviets lost the Cold War, and in practice, a group project's success is dependent on the contributions of individuals. But there is a difference between individual actions done as an individual and individual actions done as part of a group. These games teach how to be an individual and a group member at the same time.

The key to contributing to a group is to be able to notice when the group needs you to be a leader and when the group needs you to be a follower and to be able to switch back and forth quickly. A good analogy to this situation is a team sport like basketball. In basketball, a team would never win if every time each player got the ball they drove straight for the hoop. To win games, knowing when to pass is even more important than knowing how to shoot. A good player will pay attention to everyone on the court. They play unselfishly — if they get the ball and are heavily defended, they will pass to an open player. However, if they have a wide open shot, they won't pass it off — they'll take the shot.

These games will teach your players when to pass and when to take the shot. They will teach them to sense when the group needs them to take the lead and when it needs them to pass off the lead to someone else. They will learn how to be team players.

Incidentally, if you have the resources, team sports are great teachers of Dynamics. If you can, have your group play a sport such as basketball, soccer, ultimate Frisbee, jai alai — any of these games are great for getting your group to (literally) function as a team.

33. Let's Go to the Bank

Players Needed: 4 or more
Points of Concentration: Creativity, give and take,
    group awareness, support

This game is rather advanced. It basically teaches how to perform a group scene on-stage. At the same time, it offers up a hard lesson on subverting your own ideas to support your fellow players. For an improv group, this is one of the most difficult and important exercises in the book. It teaches two hard lessons: how to get a big group of people on-stage to all focus on the same task, and when to let go of your ego and stay out of a scene when you are not needed.

Before we start, a quick aside: The "correct" version of this game, which is not presented here, was invented at ImprovOlympic by a very talented teacher named Susan Messing. The description that follows is a result of me walking through Susan's class to go to the bathroom, seeing ten seconds of this game, and thinking I understood it when I decided to try it in my own class a week later. I didn't, of course; the focuses of the two versions are completely different.

I mention this for three reasons: First, so Susan doesn't get mad and sue me. Second, to acknowledge that theft and reinterpretation are responsible for a lot of growth in the world of improvisation. You could ask ten different groups around the country what a Harold is or how to play Improv Jeopardy or the Debate game, and get ten different answers. In most cases, this is a good thing; these groups take an idea and make it work for them. Which leads me to reason number three: it's an example of how the rules of improv can work in real life.

Susan has this great idea that starts with somebody yelling "Let's go to the bank!" From that initiation, she develops a great game. Cool. However, when I see Susan's idea and take it and develop it on my own, that is, when I build my own ideas on top of hers, the result is something completely different, and just as cool. Susan would not have come up with my version of this game, and I wouldn't have come up with the game at all without Susan's idea to build on. This game is an example of why the games in this book are useful. By putting two brains on the same idea, we came up with two different, and very useful exercises.

Anyhow, the game: Players spread themselves out around the space. One player (or you, the facilitator), shouts, "Let's go to the _____!", filling in the blank with any location. It can be the bank. It doesn't have to be the bank. Once the location is named, everybody shouts, "Yay!!!" as they are very excited to go to the bank or the golf course or Mars or wherever it is they're going.

At this point, everybody immediately portrays part of the environment. We will use the bank for this example. So we're at the bank, so players will become the tellers, the guard, the customers waiting in line. Players will *also* become the ATM, the velvet ropes where you wait in line, the door of the vault, etc. The players should try to create a complete picture of this location.

Once the stage picture is set, the players begin interacting as they normally would in this location. Note that the ropes and the vault door probably won't be talking, as these objects lack the power of speech.

We are now ready for the all-important Phase Three of this game. At this point, there are multiple interactions and conversations happening on-stage. The goal is to narrow the focus of the scene to showcase one particular interaction.

Now, what we *don't* want is for people to just stop what they're doing. Every idea is valuable and will eventually serve the scene. What we *do* want is for everyone to continue their interactions while making themselves aware of everyone else's interactions. Once everyone is aware of everything happening on-stage, they can decide which of the interactions should be the focus of the scene.

How is this decided, you ask? Ideally, the interaction that takes focus should be the most important interaction.

Great, you say, how do you know what's most important?

The most important thing happening on-stage has the "highest stakes," that is, the event that is most important to the people to whom the event is happening.

In the bank, the guy changing the address on his account has a lower-stakes interaction than the guy who is reporting his credit card stolen. Mr. Address Change doesn't want to miss a bank statement, but Mr. Stolen Credit Card may be responsible for paying a lot of money. Similarly, the guy who's reporting his credit card stolen has a lower-stakes interaction than the guy whose credit card was stolen, and look, check your computer, some guy is using it right now at Tiffany's, and the Porsche dealership. The first guy *may be* responsible for a lot of money, the second guy *is* responsible for a lot of money, and it's getting worse *right now*.

So the group needs to determine which is the highest-stakes interaction. If they all seem to be equal, then they should determine which interaction is loudest, or most center stage, or otherwise the most deserving of their attention. We will call this most important interaction the Primary Game.

Once it is identified, all of the players must adjust their own interactions to support the Primary Game. This means that first and foremost, the players who are not a part of the Primary Game must accept that this scene in the bank is not about them. Then, they can try to use their own interaction to support the Primary Game.

Example: In the bank, we start with the following:

Fig. 12

One player plays the bank guard by the door.
One player is trying to fill out a deposit slip, but none of the pens work.
Two players are waiting in line, talking about how slow the line is.
One player forms the ropes that form the line.
One player plays the ATM.
One player plays a teller.
One player is a bank robber, standing at the teller window.

As the game starts, the guard is whistling, Mr. Deposit Slip is complaining out loud about how none of the pens work, the people in line are talking about how they are in a hurry, the ropes and ATM are saying nothing, and the teller is asking the robber how she can help. The robber hands a note and says, "Hurry up, keep quiet, I have a gun."

With their individual roles established, all of the players now tune in to each other. The players realize that the highest-stakes interaction is the bank robbery. So they now adjust their behavior to support the Primary Game of the bank robbery. First, they become quieter, so that the bank robbery is easier to hear.

The guard notices his shoe is untied, to give the robbery more time to develop. The people in line start complaining about the robber taking so long. The ropes, the ATM, and Mr. Deposit Slip just keep quiet, as at

65

this point they don't know how to help the Primary Game along.

Eventually, the people in line complain to the teller. The teller explains, "We're being robbed!" The people in line say, "Well, hurry up, I gotta get back to work!"

At this point, the other players realize that the Primary Game has changed; it's not just a bank robbery, it's a bank robbery that nobody cares about. So, the guard says, "Yeah, hurry up, buddy, I go on break in five minutes!" Mr. Deposit Slip goes up to the robber and asks, "Hey, which pen did you write the note with? I can't find one that works."

The robber loans his pen, gets his money, and starts to leave, but as he goes, he bumps into the ropes. The person playing ropes realizes that she now can play a part, so she falls over onto the robber, tying him up until the guard can arrest him.

In this example, the scene worked because:

- Everyone started out by developing their own little bit.
- Once they knew their little part in the big picture of the bank, they paid attention to what everyone else was doing to determine who had the highest-stakes interaction.
- Those who were not directly a part of the Primary Game gave focus to the Primary Game, so it could develop. They realized that the scene was not about them. So, while they were still an important part of the environment, they didn't steal focus from the Primary Game.
- As each set of players realized how they could support and build on to the Primary Game, they took focus and made their contribution.
- The player who didn't have a good reason to join the primary game, in this case the ATM guy, simply stayed out of it. This player was still supporting the game — he added to the environment of the bank, and he also supported by not stealing focus.

Once the Primary Game has been identified and played out, one of the players on-stage edits the scene and starts a new scene by shouting, "Hey! Let's go to the _____!" with a new location. Then it starts all over. Keep the exercise going through at least four or five different locations.

Over the entire game, the players should try to make sure that everyone gets an equal share of the spotlight. For instance, the guy who played the ATM in the bank was in the background the whole time. So if possible, that player should be part of the Primary Game in the next location. This game is kind of lame if the same three people hog all the focus the whole time.

Another reason to reward Mr. ATM with the spotlight in the second location is that he actually achieved the most difficult task in the bank: he stayed out of focus because he wasn't needed. There is no place for ego in Let's Go to the Bank. The worst thing you can do in this game is to say something just because you haven't said anything in a while. Such behavior will confuse if not disrupt completely the Primary Game.

In my experience, groups learning this game will go back and forth from one extreme to the other: Initially, they'll just talk over each other the entire time, doing their own thing and ignoring everyone else. Once you try to correct that, then everyone who's not in the Primary Game will stop and just watch it, instead of continuing their environment work. So, I recommend side-coaching this exercise until they get the hang of it. When they're talking over each other, ask the group "What's most important here?" and remind them to listen to each other. If they stop what they're doing, just remind them to keep it going.

When perfected, this game will result in a series of amazing and usually hilarious group scenes that really show the power of the Group Mind. Watching a big group of players bat a fun idea around like a volleyball is very entertaining.

34. What Are You Doing? Tag Team

Players Needed: 4 or more
Points of Concentration: Give and take, energy building,
    quick thinking, focus and concentration

This game is a modification of What Are you Doing? (page 56) from last chapter. So if you skipped over it before, go back and read it. I'll wait here. What Are You Doing? Tag Team changes the focus of the game from the individual to the group. This game will be a (friendly) competition, so divide your group into two teams.

The game is played as before, with minor changes: When a violation is committed (describing the activity you're really doing, hesitating, or reusing an activity), in addition to the player moving to the back of the line, the other team gets a point.

However, a team can prevent the other team from getting a point by tagging out, like in wrestling. If Doug gets in trouble and can't think of anything to say, he may tag the hand of a player in the back line. That player then enters the game and must immediately pick up where Doug left off. (That means that if Doug says "I'm throwing ..." and then freezes up and tags out, the player tagging in will have to say what Doug was throwing.)

Hesitation is still a violation. So if Doug hesitates too long before tagging out, the other team will still get a point (you or some judge will determine when a hesitation is too long). To prevent hesitation penalties, a player from the back line can tag in. Instead of waiting for Doug, a player can notice that Doug is in trouble and rush in to replace him before he gets stuck.

The team with the most points at the end of the game wins.

The point of the game is to think as a team; the active player must be looking for the right time to step down and hand the reins over to his team; the players in the back line must be looking for the active player to need some support and jump in as soon as they are needed. Overconfidence in oneself in this game will resort in the other team getting points, so this game is especially good in teaching people who may think they have to carry the whole group that the team is actually there to support them.

35. Temptations

Players Needed: 4 to 8
Other Needs: A source of music (optional)
Points of Concentration: Group dynamics, give and take,
      group awareness

This game is not named after the sinful kind of temptations, but rather the funky kind of Temptations, meaning the R&B group. In this game, your group is going to get down old-school.

Once again, if you have more than eight people, you should split up into multiple groups.

Players stand in a line. Start the music or have the group come up with their own rhythm. The group will then start to dance.

The style of dance in this game is the fifties-backup-singer style. The archetypal move would be standing in a line, facing left, sticking your right arm out at waist level and sweeping it up and right. The other classic would be the step-forward-step-back and snap move.

Fig. 13

Fig. 14

You get the picture. But you are going to improvise moves in this style.

LEVEL 1

The player at the far left (Doug) is the leader of the line. As the dance begins, everyone in the line must follow the lead of Doug. At this point, the game is similar to Group Mirror (page 40). The goal is for the whole line to move in synch with one another. After a little bit, Doug will break into some dance move that takes him over to the far right side of the line, meaning that a new player is now on the left. That player becomes the new leader. Continue until everyone has had a chance to be the leader.

LEVEL 2

Of course, not all of these backup dancers moved in synch. There were two main types of moves: *synch*, like the ones you did in Level 1, and *stagger*. A staggered move travels down the line in a ripple. For a simple example of staggered choreography ask your group to do The Wave. To rephrase it simply: the group does *synch* moves all at once and *stagger* moves one at a time.

For Level 2, the group will do a dance using stagger moves. Similarly to Level 1, Doug will start at the left and initiate a move. This move will travel down the line. Eventually Doug will make way for a new leader.

Stagger moves require more of a sense of rhythm than synch moves. Synch moves are easy to fake and muff around with so they look OK even when they're not sharp. Stagger moves are done by one person at a time, so if that person misses a move or is late people will notice. However, the group can cover up "mistakes" by not treating them as mistakes. For example:

Doug initiates a move by spinning around and facing the back wall. On the next beat, Karen does the same. Then TJ on the next beat, then Paul on the next. So the pattern has been established that one player does a move every beat. However, when Doug spins back to face front,

Karen doesn't see it right away. So she spins to face front after two beats instead of one. Now, TJ could have also spun on that second beat, what to him would have been the "correct" beat. But if he does that, it would be obvious that Karen had missed her turn. So instead, he lets Karen spin and then waits another two beats before doing his spin. Instead of assuming that Karen had made a mistake, he assumed that what Karen did was correct, even though it was different from what he was expecting. In other words, he made Karen's incorrect move correct, by doing the same thing that she did. Then Paul finishes the pattern by waiting another two beats and spinning.

Another possibility: Doug misses the first beat and spins on the second beat. Karen also is late, so she spins three beats later. If TJ and Paul are staying aware, they can support everybody by continuing the pattern: TJ spins four beats later, Paul five.

The important things to remember in this level is that 1) each move is a part of a larger pattern and 2) everything anyone does is correct.

LEVEL 3

Now mix together Levels 1 and 2. The group may mix synch and stagger moves and must decide as they are doing the moves which kind they will be.

LEVEL 4

Same as Level 3, but now the player on the left will not always lead. Instead the group will pass the lead. Each player will have to pay attention to the piece as a whole to figure out when they should take the lead and when they should yield it to someone else. It is important that each player have the lead for an equal amount of time; one person can't dominate.

Note that people in the middle of the line will probably have to initiate synch moves, while people on the ends can start stagger moves if they wish. The group may still move around and switch the order of the line; they will have to figure out mid-dance when that should happen.

Making up a dance isn't that hard, but making up a dance that looks like it's choreographed is. The group must be tuned into each other at all times. Primarily, the players must be aware of when they should step up and take the lead and when they should stay back and just follow. The two things that cause Temptations to self-destruct are, not surprisingly, related to dynamics. The game won't work if there's a tug-of-war between two or more people, each of whom is trying to lead. It also won't work if there's no leader; at best it will be one move repeated forever. When this game is played at its best, each player can sense when the lead is about to come to them — they are aware of when Doug is going to stop leading, and they are aware of whether anyone else is already set to take it.

36. Advanced Red Light, Green Light

Players Needed: 6 to 12
Other Needs: A big open space (like a stage), a cone
or similar marker
Points of Concentration: Group awareness, give and take

Here we have another kids game modified to our uses. This exercise is tough even after the group figures out how to do it.

For those of you unfamiliar with the kids game Red Light, Green Light, here's an overview.

Red Light, Green Light

Players Needed: 3 or more
Points of Concentration: Focus and concentration, listening

Doug stands at one end of the room or stage. He is the first "spotlight." The other players line up on the other end of the room or stage. Their goal is to be the first to tag Doug.

Doug turns around so that his back is to the group and says "green light." The players then try to move forward to get to Doug.

Whenever he wants, Doug will turn around and say "red light." At this point, if Doug sees a player moving, he sends that player back to the start line. During the red light, players must stay frozen. They can move again when Doug turns back around and says "green light." The first player to touch Doug becomes the next spotlight.

Spotlights should keep the players off balance by varying the length of the red and green lights.

Depending on how difficult you want the game to be, select one of the following definitions of "moving," for which a player will be sent back to start:

Easy: Moving the feet
Medium: Moving the feet; also, any forward motion

71

(including leaning forward)
Hard: Any motion at all

For Advanced Red Light Green Light, we will take the basic concept and warp it.

The stoplight stands at one end of the room facing the rest of the group. He will face the group for the entire game. The rest of the group stands at the other end of the room. Place the cone a little more than halfway between the stoplight and the group, to indicate a sort of fifty-yard line.

LEVEL 1

The goal of the entire group is to have any one of its members reach the Stoplight. So this is a group game, not an individual game. In order to do so, they must obey the following rules:

- The group cannot speak to each other.
- The entire group must reach the fifty-yard line before any one member can cross the fifty-yard line.
- At all times, exactly one member of the group must be moving forward or backwards, and exactly one member of the group must be moving sideways.

The stoplight will call "green light" to tell the group to begin. If the stoplight sees any violation of the rules, he will call "red light" and *the entire group* must start over at the start line. Once the group is reset at the start line, the stoplight will give another green light, and the game continues.

Some possible violations:

- Two people moving forward at the same time.
- Two people moving sideways at the same time
- No one moving forward, sideways, or at all.
- Someone crossing the fifty-yard line before everyone has reached it.

This game functions as a sort of moving version of the game One to Twenty. The group must check in with each other, looking at each other, to see when they are needed to move and when they should hold still. If someone moves too quickly or impulsively, someone else will be moving and the group will have to start over.

LEVEL 2

Eventually, your group will figure out the way to achieve Level 1, which is this: (don't tell them)

One player will move back and forth right at the start line, until every other player has advanced to the fifty-yard line. Then, one of the players at the fifty-yard line will move sideways, as the player from the back walks all the way to the stoplight.

So for Level 2, we won't let them do that. Add the following two rules:

- A player must stop at the fifty-yard line; that is, when you first reach the fifty-yard line, you must freeze and let someone else move before you can move again.
- While a particular player is moving in a particular direction (either forward/backward or sideways), only two players may move in the other direction. For example, say Doug starts out moving side to side. While Doug moves sideways, Karen moves forward to the fifty-yard line. When Karen stops, Ali moves forward to the fifty-yard line. At this point, Doug must stop moving for another player to move forward. Since a player must always be moving forward, three players will have to act at once: Doug must stop moving sideways, another player will have to start moving sideways, and a third player (or Doug) will have to start moving forward.

Again, the stoplight will call "red light" if anyone breaks the rules. Let whoever reaches the stoplight become the next stoplight, or pick the person in the group who seems to have the best understanding of the game and make her be the stoplight, so the group will have to do it without her.

This may or may not come up, but you don't need to be hard-core tough on the "no one moving" violation. I tell my stoplights to give the group a "one-count" (about half a second) to realize that someone has stopped and to get the next person in motion.

This exercise is particularly good for groups that are more intellectual or focused on "problem-solving." Corporate groups in particular respond well to this kind of exercise. So if you work with a corporate group, use this exercise. If you don't work with a corporate group, go out and find one.

37. The Tag Out Game

Players Needed: 3 or more
Points of Concentration: Listening, agreement, focus and
    concentration, support, creation

Charna Halpern is the Godmother of improvisation. She started the ImprovOlympic theater, and with her partner, the late Del Close, she laid the foundation for long-form improvisation as we know it. She, Del, and Kim "Howard" Johnson wrote a book called *Truth in Comedy* that gives the basics of I.O.-style improv, including the improvisation form "The Harold" that Charna mentions. If this stuff interests you, you might want to check it out. In the meantime, Charna has donated to this book a game that she has recently started to use in her beginning improv classes, called The Tag Out.

Charna calls this a performance piece, and it is; however, I'm calling it a game, since game sounds less intimidating than performance piece. You can call it whatever you want to. This game incorporates almost every point of concentration from the whole book, so it's a great one to build to or finish with. The greatest thing about The Tag Out is that the rules of the game are simple enough for anyone to pick up, and once a group gets going, they can create a really sophisticated, complex piece. A group usually leaves The Tag Out impressed with themselves for creating such a cool, fun thing. It's great to leave a workshop or rehearsal with a group feeling so confident.

And now, ladies and gentlemen, Charna Halpern ...

The Tag Out Exercise and Performance Piece

ImprovOlympic is famous for teaching long-form improvisation, so naturally, when new students start their classes they are eager to jump in and try their hands at it. Of course, it's very difficult without first learning the basic principles of learning and remembering, agreement, and building on each other's ideas. So, to help my students learn these lessons quickly, I developed an exercise that only succeeds when these principles are followed. The piece is based on a technique we use in our Harolds, which is called a tag out.

How a Tag Out Is Used

A Harold starts off with three different improvised scenes. Over the course of the Harold, each of these scenes will return, showing the relationship of the characters at different points in time. Also, the scenes will connect and weave together. The Tag Out can be used to help achieve both of these goals: it can help heighten and explore an individual relationship or scene; it can also help connect different scenes together.

Here's an example of how The Tag Out can be used to heighten an individual scene.

Two players start by improvising a scene between a father and son. In the scene, the father is accusing the son of doing drugs. He says to his son, "I'm going to find out who's been giving you drugs if I have to go to every person in this city!"

A third actor taps the son on the shoulder and takes his place on-stage, thus "tagging him out." The new actor says, "Well, Mr. Wilson, I let the boys come next door to play basketball in my driveway, but I certainly don't give them drugs!"

A fourth actor tags out the next door neighbor and says, "As the principal of Hill High School, I assure you that there are no drug problems here!"

A fifth actor tags out the principal and says, "I sell to lots of kids. How do I know which one's yours?"

Finally, the actor who played the son tags out the drug dealer and says, "See? I didn't do it!" and the scene continues on from there. Using the tag out, we have sent the father all around the city in a matter of seconds!

You should notice a few things about how The Tag Out works. First of all, when a tag out is used, the actor who is not tagged out always remains the same character, so that there's no confusion about what's being heightened. Second, when a tag out is used, it always indicates a jump in time and space. In other words, the scene following the tag out shows the character who is not tagged out in a different place talking to a different person.

A good tag out is based on a strong one-line initiation (which is another reason I teach it to beginning classes). We should know from a character's first line who he is and what new information he is bringing to the table.

If this were part of a Harold, the neighbor, principal, and drug dealer would probably never be seen again, as they were created just to heighten one idea. However, when a tag out is used to connect scenes together, we may see characters that already exist. Here's an example of how the tag out can be used to connect scenes together:

Two players improvise a scene in which a manager is interviewing a woman in his office for a job at McDonald's. He tells her, "Working the grill is a big responsibility, so you must be reliable. The last employee I had at the grill wasn't as careful as he needed to be, so I had to fire him."

At this point the actor who played the son in our previous example now tags out the woman. He returns as the drug-crazed son, this time working the grill, messing up, and perhaps setting himself on fire. The manager, realizing that he is no longer in his office but at the grill, catches the son messing up and fires him. The woman then tags out the son again and returns to the interview. The scene continues, and both the father-son scene and the manager-employee scene have been furthered by new information.

A tag out doesn't always have to end with a return to the original scene. For example, a third player could tag out the manager after he fires the son and initiate a scene between the son and one of his friends, by saying, "Don't feel bad, dude. I got fired from Wendy's for drinking Frosties straight out of the machine." Then their scene could continue, as we learn what the son does with his friends at night. However, you will find that it is usually very satisfying to eventually return to the original scene.

A third way the tag out can be used is to show the truth about what really happened in some situation. An example would be a woman asking her boyfriend why he stood her up for their date the night before. He tells her that he was so exhausted from studying all day for the bar exam that he fell asleep. A second woman tags out the girlfriend and begins making out with the boy. The girlfriend quickly tags out the second woman and continues the scene with, "Well, I guess I can't get mad if you were studying so hard." The second woman made the boyfriend a liar with a quick tag out.

It is important to note that some tag outs are very quick, like the previous example. So, after actors are tagged out, they must stay on their toes, so that they can come right back into the piece at the right time. This also means that the actors must stay in tune with each other to decide whether to let the run of tag outs continue for a while or whether to return to the previous scene immediately.

Using this tag out idea, I created a form to not only teach tag outs but also to reinforce the idea of scenes returning in spans of time. This form is now performed brilliantly at the I.O. West theater in L.A. by the group Beer Shark Mice.

The Tag Out Performance Piece

In this piece, a story is created entirely by tag outs. A tag out is the only way to enter the piece. Usually, each actor will only play one character throughout the piece. The actors need to stay on their toes and be ready to return often and at any time. When characters return, it will rarely be in a place or time that we've seen them before. This is *not* a linear piece.

For a suggestion, I usually ask for a line of poetry. This suggestion is just something to "let hang in the air." It is not the opening line, nor is it the theme of the first scene. It's just an idea to inspire us as a group and affect the piece overall.

The first scene begins with two characters. This scene should be allowed to go on for a while, because the more information the scene generates, the more ideas the other players will have to build the story. A third player will edit the first scene by tagging out one of the players, From that point on, everyone will need to stay on their toes, listening carefully and looking for ways to build on the ideas that the group has created.

Here is an example of how a Tag Out piece might go:

Scene 1:

Doug and Karen play a man walking a woman home after their first date. After a while:

KAREN: Well, tonight was ... interesting. I thought I would hate greyhound racing. And I was right.

DOUG: It's still early. Let's go get a drink.

KAREN: No thanks, I'm really tired.

DOUG: Hey, that dinner was expensive. At least we could make out for a while. *(BOB tags out KAREN.)*

Scene 2

BOB: Wow. She actually punched you in the face?

DOUG: I never saw it coming. That girl was crazy!

BOB: You know, none of my other roommates ever get beat up on dates. Maybe it's you.

DOUG: What? No way. I'm a perfect gentleman. *(MARY tags out BOB.)*

Scene 3

MARY: How dare you insult my weight like that!

DOUG: Hey, sorry! I thought you were pregnant! *(MARY slaps DOUG. ALEXANDRA tags out MARY.)*

Scene 4
ALEXANDRA: You pig!
DOUG: What? I'm just saying that chick was hot! *(ALEXANDRA slaps DOUG. REBECCA tags out ALEXANDRA.)*

Scene 5
DOUG: Can you pay for this? *(REBECCA slaps DOUG. KIM tags out REBECCA.)*

Scene 6
(KIM slaps DOUG.)
DOUG: I didn't even say anything yet! *(BOB tags out KIM.)*

Back to Scene 2
DOUG: Do you really think it's me?
BOB: You gotta learn how to treat women right. You gotta talk nice to them and give them flowers. Tell them they're pretty and that you like to cook. That's what women want. *(STUART tags out BOB.)*

Scene 7
STUART: Well, Doug, your mother liked me because I was a fireman. Women love firemen. You should treat a woman like you're saving her from a burning building. *(KIM tags out STUART.)*

Back to Scene 6
(KIM and slaps DOUG. STUART tags out KIM.)

Back to Scene 7
STUART: Like the *building's* on fire, not like *she's* on fire!
DOUG: So I shouldn't have made her stop, drop, and roll? *(NICK tags out STUART.)*

Scene 8
NICK: Doug, my man, you listen to ol' Stubby Fingers Magee. Lovin' a woman is just like playin' the saxophone. You gotta be gentle, hit all the right notes, and listen to the music that she's making. *(BILL tags out DOUG.)*

Scene 9

BILL: Stubby Fingers Magee, you listen to ol' Blind Lemon Samuels. Playing the saxophone is just like lovin' a woman. You got to be gentle ... *(REBECCA tags out NICK.)*

Scene 10

REBECCA: We've got good news, Mr. Samuels. Your tests have come back, and you will regain your sight. You're not blind.

BILL: Oh, doctor, this is terrible! I can't be a famous jazz musician if I'm not blind!

(The scene continues for a while between BLIND LEMON and his DOCTOR. MARY tags out BILL.)

Scene 11 (connects to Scene 3)

MARY: Doctor, I think I might be pregnant ...

... and the piece continues, following the characters around and heightening the themes of love and respect, image versus reality, and any other themes that arise.

Let's take a look at some of the moves that our players made in this example.

Scene 1 would obviously be longer than the example to develop more themes and information for us to explore. This led us to scene 2, where we jump in time to later that night, after the date. This allows us to leave the violence at the end of the date to the imagination of the audience.

In the middle of scene 2, after Doug says that he's a perfect gentleman, we see a series of quick scenes (scenes 3-6) showing that, in fact, he is not. A quick series of scenes like this that heightens one idea is called a *run*. At the end of the run, we returned to scene 2.

Later in the scene, we left on another run showing Doug asking various people for advice. But during this run, the players decided not to return to scene 2 and instead created a transition to another scene. Once we realize that we are expanding our world to find a new relationship, we have left the run and are now creating a *chain*. The chain (scenes 8 and 9) takes us to scene 10. Rebecca had appeared in the piece once before, as one of the unlucky dates. However her appearance as the date was very short and functional. So Rebecca is free to enter as a different character.

When Mary appears in the doctor's office in scene 11, she decides that she will play her character from scene 3 in the earlier run. So Mary makes a connection: she has caused the chain of scenes to loop back around on itself.

Once the piece is underway, it's fine to add additional moves and break the rules a bit. If it is important for a character to join a scene without tagging anyone out, he may do so. Then, if another player wants to do a scene alone with the main character, he can just tag out two people instead of one. I have seen scenes where a group of people are in the piece, such as a classroom scene, and a person initiated a tag out just by waving the whole class away. Sometimes two actors may realize that the story demands that they do a scene together without any other characters. In that case, they can just walk on-stage in front of the previous scene and begin their own, signaling to the previous scene that they have been edited. These are the same editing techniques that we use in the Harold, as described in my book *Truth in Comedy*.

Party Games

These games are, by and large, all-encompassing group exercises. Most of them have physical and mental aspects, valuing speed and accuracy. They reward both manual dexterity and mental acuity. And for some reason, I learned most of them in my church youth group in high school.

These games are fun. They are fun party games that can be played recreationally. It just so happens that they are also great group-bonding games.

38. Thumper

Players Needed: 5 or more
Points of Concentration: Energy, focus and concentration

This game is similar to George (page 82)/The Name Game (page 19), with several notable differences.

LEVEL 1
First of all, instead of clapping, everyone keeps a drum roll going constantly by slapping their hands on their knees. To begin each round, one person leads the following:

DOUG: What's the name of the game?
EVERYONE: Thumper!
DOUG: Why do we play it?
EVERYONE: To get warmed up! (Yes, *warmed* up. That is why we
        are playing it.)

Doug will then begin by making a sound and a motion. The sound will somehow include Doug's name. For example, he could pretend to hold a trumpet to his mouth and say (to the tune of the ballpark "charge" song) "Doo-doo-doo! Doo-doo-doo! Doug!" Anything sound and motion is good; the bigger, louder, and/or dumber the better.

After Doug makes his sound and motion, the person to Doug's right makes a sound and motion including their own name. This continues around the circle until every player has a sound and motion.

When focus gets back to Doug, he begins, a la The Name Game, using each person's sound-and-motion in place of their name. So to

81

start, Doug makes his own noise, then someone else's. Then that person makes their own noise, then someone else's, etc.

When someone messes up, you have two options. If you are focusing on Energy, just start over with another big drum roll, and the above call-and-response. If you are focusing on Focus, penalize that player by having the group assign them a new, and presumably less flattering, sound-and-motion that they must use for the remainder of the game.

LEVEL 2
Gradually, as the game progresses, phase the names out of the sound-and-motion, so that the game becomes a series of silly noises.

39. George

Players Needed: 6 or more
Points of Concentration: Focus and concentration

This game is a li'l devil. It combines The Three-Four Rhythm (page 33) with The Name Game (page 19).

Players stand in a circle, noting the spot on the floor where they stand. Choose one player, who will start off the clapping. During the game, this player will be called George instead of his real name. (If you have a player who is really named George, use him. Or her, if it's George Sand. Or, if you have two players with the same first name, I'd recommend using one of them.)

George will count off the three-four clap, "one, two, three," then the group will start up the rhythm. Once the group is up and running, George will initiate The Name Game by saying his own name, "George," on the *down* clap (the first beat, where each player has one palm facing down, one up). He will then say another player's name on the *out* clap (Palms facing away, clapping with neighbors). The normal clap is a rest.

The person who George named must then say their own name on the *down*, and someone else's name on the *out*. And so on. A person messes up if:

They don't say their own name on the very next *down* clap;
They don't say someone else's name on the very next *out* clap;
They try to use George's real name; or
They screw up the clapping.

When someone messes up, you have two options:

LEVEL 1

The person who messed up switches places in the circle with George. While the players switch positions in the circle, their names do not. So, if Mike messes up, he switches places with George. For the next round of the game, Mike will start the game and respond to "George;" George will respond to "Mike." Every time someone messes up they become George, and whoever was George takes their name.

LEVEL 2

Consider George as the top position in the circle. The player to George's right (let's say it's Mike again) is the lowest point. When someone messes up, they leave their spot to become Mike. Everyone below the messee slides up one slot and responds to the name of the person who was formerly in that spot. Again, the names never move; only the people standing in those spots do.

An example:

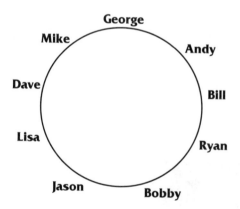

Let's say Ryan can't handle it and goofs up. Ryan now becomes Mike, Mike becomes Dave, Dave becomes Lisa, Lisa becomes Jason, Jason becomes Bobby, and Bobby becomes Ryan. Bill, Andy, and George don't change names.

This version adds a little competition into the mix, because you could say that whoever is George at the end of the game wins.

40. Bibbity Bibbity Bop

Players Needed: 6 or more
Points of Concentration: Focus and concentration

This game is a ton of fun, but it gets pretty complicated, so take this one slow until you get the hang of it. The object of the game is to not be in the middle of the circle.

LEVEL 1

Players stand in a circle with Doug in the middle. Doug will go up to a person on the outside of the circle and say one of two things: "bibbity bibbity bop" or "bop."

If Doug says "bibbity bibbity bop," Karen must say "bop" before Doug does, or she becomes the player in the middle. If both say "bop" at the same time, the person on the outside stays on the outside.

If Doug says "bop," Karen can't say anything, or she becomes the player in the middle.

The other players serve as judges in close calls. One thing to watch for in this game: often, players in the middle will just say "bibbity bibbity," and wait for the other person to say "bop." If this happens, remind them that they won't be able to say "bop" before the other player if they don't say "bop" at all.

LEVEL 2

After the group has the hang of Level 1, start to add in images. Images involve three people on the outside of the circle: the person pointed to by the player in the middle and the people to either side of him. The first image is "elephant." Doug points at someone and says, "elephant!" and then counts out loud to ten. The person pointed to must

stick their left arm straight out like a trunk, wrap their right arm around their left arm, and touch their nose with their right hand. The people on either side must use their arms to form elephant ears on the first player's head. It looks like this:

Fig. 15

If any one of these three people don't get into the proper position by the time the player in the middle reaches ten, that person goes into the middle. The counter is encouraged to count as fast as he can as long as the numbers are understandable.

Fig. 16

LEVEL 3:

Start adding more and more images. Some classics are kamikaze: The center player makes Junior Birdman goggles by making "OK" signs with both hands, then putting them upside-down on his face, so that he is looking through the O, and his fingers are on his cheeks. The players on the sides form wings.

Fig. 17

Convoy: The player in the middle drives a big steering wheel and honks the horn; players to the side crouch down and become wheels, moving their arms around in circles to simulate movement.

Fig. 18

Angels: The classic *Charlie's Angels* pose, but I give all three of them guns. Person in the center holds the gun up at head level; players on the sides kneel and aim out. If your want to get technical, it's walkie-talkie in the center, gun on the left, and karate stance on the right.

Aria: Person in the middle leans forward and sings a beautiful high note. Players on the side grab center person's arms and hold him up so he doesn't fall on his face.

Fig. 19

Viking: Person in the middle makes horns on his helmet. Players on the side are rowing the boat.

There are tons more images out there. After you learn these, make up your own images!

Fig. 20

41. Fuzzy Duck

Players Needed: 4 or more
Points of Concentration: Energy building, focus and concentration

The key to this game is speed. See how fast you can go. The fringe benefit of this game is that when someone messes up, they often do so by saying a swear word.

In Fuzzy Duck, everyone stands in a circle. The focus will be passed from person to person along the circle. If the focus is traveling counter-clockwise, you pass the focus by turning to the person to your right and saying, "fuzzy duck." If the focus is traveling clockwise, you pass the focus by turning to the person to your left and saying, "ducky fuzz." Anyone can, when the focus comes to them, reverse the direction that the focus is traveling by saying, "Duzzy?" (Pronounced "Does he?")

Again, try to move the focus as fast as possible. Stop only to laugh when people accidentally cuss.

42. Vroom

Players Needed: 6 or more
Points of Concentration: Energy building, focus and concentration

This game is similar to Fuzzy Duck (page 86), but with less sex and more violence. The sound passed around the circle is "vroom," like a race car, the more realistic the better. When players pass the vroom, they should also add to the illusion of great speed by pointing with both hands as if a very fast Formula One car just sped by, and they were pointing at it. (Actually, they'll be pointing at the person they pass the Vroom to.) Get that Vroom going fast before adding the next noise.

The next noise is the sound of screeching tires, accompanied by an X formed with both arms. A Screech will reverse the direction of the Vroom around the circle. You can't Screech a Screech; there must be at least one Vroom between Screeches. Play this level for a while, then add the third sound.

The third noise is "turbo!" accompanied by a look up. A Turbo, much like the turbo boost of KITT from *Knight Rider*, keeps the Vroom moving in the same direction, but jumps into the air, skipping over the next person in the circle. Play continues in the same direction when the focus

car lands at the second person away from the one who said "turbo!"

People usually figure this out, but a Turbo can be followed by a Turbo or a Screech, as well as a Vroom. If a Turbo is followed by a Screech, the focus goes to the person the Turbo leapt over, in the opposite direction.

Fig. 21

43. Zoom Schwartz Profigliano

Players Needed: 6 or more
Points of Concentration: Energy building, focus and concentration

This is another pass-the-focus game. Players stand in a circle. They may pass the focus around using the following moves:

Zoom passes the focus to whoever the player points at;

Elvis passes the focus to the person to the player's left;
Profigliano passes the focus to the person to the player's right.

In addition, when someone tries to pass the focus to a player, that player may say *Schwartz*. This blocks the pass, in essence, and the person who tried to pass must then try to pass it to someone else. A Schwartz may be used to respond to a Zoom, an Elvis, or a Profigliano; however, you can't Schwartz a Schwartz; if someone blocks your move, you can't block it back at them.

This game can get going pretty fast. For added excitement, add the command *Shuffle*, which causes everyone to scramble their arrangement in the circle, forming a new circle.

Conclusion

Hopefully, you have brought these games and exercises to your group and one of two things have happened: either they had such a great time that they bonded or they had such a terrible time that they bonded. It is now up to you to continue to create an atmosphere that continues to support a happy group experience.

Continue with bonding opportunities. There are a lot of things that you can do that aren't exercises out of a book. There are two general categories of bonding opportunities: shared experiences and working for a common goal.

A shared experience could be going to see a movie, a museum, or a baseball game together. The best bonding experience I've ever been a part of was when the director of a show I was in hired a limousine to just drive the cast around Chicago for an hour. It was a nice surprise and something we all got to do together. Shared experiences could also consist of each individual sharing something with the group. My company, Baby Wants Candy, has "Film Night" every Christmas where each member brings in a videotape of themselves in an embarrassing commercial, a play from high school, or a home movie, and we just laugh at each other.

Working for a common goal means things like playing basketball or softball together. Do a fundraising walk or volunteer at a soup kitchen. Decorate the office together. Heck, even helping somebody move would fall into this category. See if you can work that one out. "By carrying my couch up three flights of stairs, you're helping the group!"

The key to a shared experience or a common goal is that the experience being shared should not be too closely related to whatever your group works on most of the time. You are giving your group members something to talk about besides your work, which will get your group more relaxed and comfortable with each other.

One thought: Research your group before you suggest an activity, so you don't put someone in the awkward position of not wanting to do something but also not wanting to say no to it. For example, make sure no one in your group has a mortal fear of heights before you sign everyone up for the skydiving trip. A well-known theater company had a bonding exercise in which the cast turned off the lights and finger-painted on each other with glow-in-the-dark body paint. This would be a good example of something to make sure everyone's comfortable with before you break it out. If they're into it, hey, go for it.

A general principle for maintaining a successful group environment:

It is not important that everyone in your group likes each other. However, it is essential that everyone in your group respects each other.

In one of my improv groups, one of my least favorite people to hang out with was my favorite person to do scenes with. That team was very successful, and we really enjoyed working together, because we all respected each other. It is your job as a group facilitator to make sure that everyone has an opportunity to shine and to earn the respect of their teammates.

The key to respect is to make each member important in their own way. This will keep everyone on something of an equal level. Try to find something for each member of the group to be in charge of. For example, say you are the director of a play, and it is fairly obvious to you that one of your cast members can't act as well as everybody else. It is your job to find a way to use that person's strengths, so that they still contribute to the whole and get the respect of their castmates. Maybe that means that you put this person in charge of planning the cast party or making the pre-show tape. Find their strength and make sure that they look good. Similarly, if someone is head and shoulders above the rest of the group in terms of acting talent, put them in charge of something humble like making a phone tree or collecting laundry.

Finally, never underestimate the power of fun. Sometimes the best thing you can do for a group is to just let them blow off steam by doing something completely unproductive but incredibly fun. Run around outside and play tag. Do a rehearsal wearing inappropriate costumes and hats. Go on a secret raid to steal all of the staplers from accounts payable. Just have fun.

About the Author

Peter Gwinn began improvising with the group Cujokra at Carleton College and has never stopped. He came to Chicago's world-renowned ImprovOlympic theater in 1990, where he worked with Charna Halpern and Del Close. Peter started performing at ImprovOlympic theater in 1990 and teaching there in 1994. He currently performs with ImprovOlympic theater's resident company, Baby Wants Candy, who have performed to sell-out crowds in Chicago, New York, Edinburgh, and Singapore. Peter lives in Chicago with his lovely wife Emily.

Truth in Comedy
The manual of improvisation
CHARNA HALPERN, DEL CLOSE & KIM "HOWARD" JOHNSON
foreword by MIKE MYERS
paper 5½" x 8½" (Photos) 160 pages · ISBN 1-56608-003-7
Order #B164

Who would have ever thought that learning the finer points of improvisation could be such fun? The "Harold," an innovative improvisational tool, helped *Saturday Night Live's* Mike Myers and Chris Farley, George Wendt ("Norm" on *Cheers*) and many other actors on the road to TV and film stardom. Now it is described fully in this new book for the benefit of other would-be actors and comics. The "Harold" is a form of competitive improv involving six or seven players. They take a theme suggestion from the audience and "free associate" on the theme into a series of rapid-fire one-liners that build into totally unpredictable skits with hilarious results. The teams compete with scoring based on applause. The "Harold" is a fun way to "loosen up" and learn to think quickly, build continuity, develop characterizations and sharpen humor — all part of successful improvising.

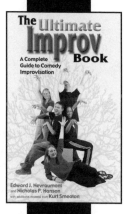

The Ultimate Improv Book
A complete guide to comedy improvisation
EDWARD J. NEVRAUMONT, NICHOLAS P. HANSON
with additional material by KURT SMEATON
paper 5½" x 8½" 280 pages · ISBN 1-56608-075-4
Order #B248

This comprehensive manual shows the who, what, when, why and how of comedy improvisation. It is a complete improv curriculum program divided into twenty-four class-length units. *The book is divided into four parts including:* **Introduction** explains what improv is and how to create an improv team. **Improv Skills** shows some basic rules, physicalization, characterization, teamwork, use of suggestion. **Structuring** describes who, what and how to make improv structures. **Strategies** gives hints and tips for evaluating performance and putting on a show. Unlike other improv books, this book provides the tools to start an improv team or club at your school. Includes a lesson plan and a unique section that shows how to structure and create your own new improv games. Also includes appendices with many games and exercises.

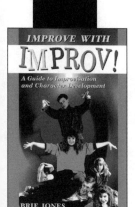

Improve with Improv!
A guide to improvisation and character development
BRIE JONES
paper 5½" x 8½" 144 pages · ISBN 0-916260-98-4
Order #B160

This book is a complete improv curriculum program divided into twenty class-length workshops. Each workshop contains carefully selected exercises designed to help students focus on one aspect of a character's personality. Students learn how to create characters from their own imaginations through the use of solo and ensemble pantomime, physicalization, vocal techniques, props and more. Gestures, facial expressions, voice and body language are studied in isolation. Many ensemble sketches are included, along with a final improv sketch with enough "roles" for all members of a large class. Also includes class syllabus and guidelines, character outline sheet to duplicate, character examples, and a recommended reading list.

Order Form

Meriwether Publishing Ltd.
PO Box 7710
Colorado Springs CO 80933-7710
Phone: 800-937-5297 Fax: 719-594-9916
Website: www.meriwether.com

Please send me the following books:

_____ **Group Improvisation BK-B259**   **$15.95**
by Peter Gwinn with additional material by Charna Halpern
The manual of ensemble improv games

_____ **Truth in Comedy #BK-B164**   **$17.95**
by Charna Halpern, Del Close and Kim "Howard" Johnson
The manual of improvisation

_____ **Theatre Games for Young Performers**   **$16.95**
#BK-B188
by Maria C. Novelly
Improvisations and exercises for developing acting skills

_____ **Comedy Improvisation #BK-B175**   **$14.95**
by Delton T. Horn
Improv structures and exercises for actors

_____ **Acting Games — Improvisations and**   **$16.95**
Exercises #BK-B168
by Marsh Cassady
A textbook of theatre games and improvisations

_____ **Improve with Improv! #BK-B160**   **$14.95**
by Brie Jones
A guide to improvisation and character development

_____ **The Ultimate Improv Book #BK-B248**   **$16.95**
by Edward J. Nevraumont, Nicholas P. Hanson and Kurt Smeaton
A complete guide to comedy improvisation

These and other fine Meriwether Publishing books are available at your local bookstore or direct from the publisher. Prices subject to change without notice. Check our website or call for current prices.

Name: _____ e-mail: _____

Organization name: _____

Address: _____

City: _____ State: _____

Zip: _____ Phone: _____

❑ **Check enclosed**

❑ **Visa / MasterCard / Discover #** _____

Signature: _____ Expiration date: _____
            (required for credit card orders)

Colorado residents: Please add 3% sales tax.
Shipping: Include $3.95 for the first book and 75¢ for each additional book ordered.

❑ *Please send me a copy of your complete catalog of books and plays.*

Order Form

Meriwether Publishing Ltd.
PO Box 7710
Colorado Springs CO 80933-7710
Phone: 800-937-5297 Fax: 719-594-9916
Website: www.meriwether.com

Please send me the following books:

_____ **Group Improvisation BK-B259**   **$15.95**
by Peter Gwinn with additional material by Charna Halpern
The manual of ensemble improv games

_____ **Truth in Comedy #BK-B164**   **$17.95**
by Charna Halpern, Del Close and Kim "Howard" Johnson
The manual of improvisation

_____ **Theatre Games for Young Performers**   **$16.95**
#BK-B188
by Maria C. Novelly
Improvisations and exercises for developing acting skills

_____ **Comedy Improvisation #BK-B175**   **$14.95**
by Delton T. Horn
Improv structures and exercises for actors

_____ **Acting Games — Improvisations and**   **$16.95**
Exercises #BK-B168
by Marsh Cassady
A textbook of theatre games and improvisations

_____ **Improve with Improv! #BK-B160**   **$14.95**
by Brie Jones
A guide to improvisation and character development

_____ **The Ultimate Improv Book #BK-B248**   **$16.95**
by Edward J. Nevraumont, Nicholas P. Hanson and Kurt Smeaton
A complete guide to comedy improvisation

**These and other fine Meriwether Publishing books are available at
your local bookstore or direct from the publisher. Prices subject to
change without notice. Check our website or call for current prices.**

Name: _____ e-mail: _____

Organization name: _____

Address: _____

City: _____ State: _____

Zip: _____ Phone: _____

□ **Check enclosed**

□ **Visa / MasterCard / Discover #** _____

Expiration
Signature: _____   *date:* _____
(required for credit card orders)

Colorado residents: Please add 3% sales tax.
Shipping: Include $3.95 for the first book and 75¢ for each additional book ordered.

□ *Please send me a copy of your complete catalog of books and plays.*